DUDLEY PUBL

D1348134

The loan of this book may be renewed .. ...
readers, by contacting the library from which it was borrowed

30 A. R 2019

a Mother's
Love

000002001434

Without
a Mother's
Love

How I Overcame the Haunting Memory
of Witnessing my Mother's Murder

AMANDA WRIGHT
WITH KATY WEITZ

JOHN BLAKE

Published by John Blake Publishing Ltd,
3 Bramber Court, 2 Bramber Road,
London W14 9PB, England

www.johnblakebooks.com

www.facebook.com/johnblakebooks
twitter.com/jblakebooks

This edition published in 2016

ISBN: 978 1 78418 984 6

All rights reserved. No part of this publication may be reproduced,
stored in a retrieval system, or transmitted in any form or by any means,
without the prior permission in writing of the publisher, nor be otherwise
circulated in any form of binding or cover other than that in which it is
published and without a similar condition including this condition
being imposed on the subsequent purchaser.

British Library Cataloguing-in-Publication Data:

A catalogue record for this book is available from the British Library.

Design by www.envydesign.co.uk

DUDLEY LIBRARIES		
000002001434		
Askews & Holts	16-May-2016	
	£7.99	
NE		

The text and other copyright material in this book remain the property of the author as the author of this work in accordance with the Copyright, Designs and Patents Act 1988.

Papers used by John Blake Publishing are natural, recyclable products made from wood grown in sustainable forests. The manufacturing processes conform to the environmental regulations of the country of origin.

Every attempt has been made to contact the relevant copyright-holders,
but some were unobtainable. We would be grateful if the
appropriate people could contact us.

Suffer we must never do
If to ourselves we are true
And admit the feelings deep inside
The very ones we try to hide.

Susan Lowson

CONTENTS

PROLOGUE

This is not a sad story. This is a story of hope and survival. I feel so lucky to be here to share my story, lucky that I did not die that day in March 1980, the day that my mother's life was so cruelly taken from her. Yes, I am here and at forty years old I have a loving husband, two beautiful daughters and a wonderful job that brings me enormous joy. Today I am in a good place. I walk down the street and I am confident enough to hold my head up, to look people in the eye and smile. I am not fearful of every stranger, not frightened of the unknown.

It wasn't always this way. There was a time, not that long ago, when I couldn't look people in the eye. I didn't realise that when strangers smiled at me in the street it was from genuine warmth. All my life I wore a cloak of suspicion and mistrust – I suppose you could say it was only to be expected after what happened, after John Dickinson took my mother's life and everything I knew. In one cruel morning, he snatched away everything that was real, solid and dependable. And I could never trust that it wouldn't happen again.

That is what they don't tell you about 'bad things'. Bad things don't just happen to a person; they *change* a person. The bad thing that happened to me at four years old changed everything about the world I knew, but it also changed me from the inside, it made me uncertain of the future. From that time onwards I carried a hard little stone of dread in my stomach, a feeling that often threatened to overwhelm me when I least expected it. The worst thing imaginable had happened to me. Who could say it wouldn't happen again? Who knew what the future held? I didn't. Nobody did, and so nothing could reassure me that my life would turn out okay. I learned from a young age never to take certainty for granted again.

John Dickinson didn't just take my mother from me: he took away my belief in a positive future. From that time onwards I had trouble sleeping, I felt constantly worried and anxious. Who knew what was around the corner? I was always waiting for something to go wrong. So I tried to second-guess people and situations, to work out how every little change affected me and my future. Today, it's not as bad as it used to be and I've learned to relax a little more around my children, to encourage their independence instead of fearing the unknown. But that sense of standing at the edge of a cliff and waiting, just waiting to fall, hasn't left me completely. There are still mornings when I wake up bathed in sweat, cold dread flooding my body, my stormy mind plagued by worry: *Something is going to go wrong. What is going to go wrong?* Nowadays I breathe deeply, look over at the body of my husband Glen sleeping next to me, peaceful and relaxed, and I feel reassured. Then the anxiety fades and my normal mind returns and takes over. I can think and breathe again and I start to mentally list all the things I have to do that day. Energy returns to my mind and body. I jump up out of bed, ready and eager to start the day. It's like a pistol has gone off in my head and BANG! I just want to get going.

There is still so much I want to do, still so much I want to see, experience and achieve. Will I manage to get it all done? I don't know. Don't get me wrong – I'm not hugely ambitious. I have been in the same job for seventeen years now, running a local after-school Fun Club. But I have hopes and dreams the same as everyone else – sometimes they are modest dreams, but still, I reach for them every day. I set myself goals and I try to be the best I can be in all areas of my life. I'm proud and pleased with what I have achieved so far but I'm not stopping now.

What is it all about? That feeling of urgency that takes over every morning, that sense of wanting to get out into the world and burn through the day like a comet. What is it?

It is not simply about being a 'success' in my work life: it is more than that. It's about living a good life, a happy life, and a worthwhile life. Doing all those things my mother never had the chance to do. Doing the things I know she would have wished for me. We live in a modest three-bedroom house in Stevenage; Glen is a tiler and our two daughters are kind, healthy and happy children. We are close to our neighbours, I have good friends and family, and every now and then we treat ourselves to a special family holiday, where we can enjoy quality time together. I like to keep fit, I try to help people and make others happy. I laugh a lot and often. This is what makes for a good life.

Over the years I have pieced together what happened to Mum and me on that morning on 4 March 1980. Like a very slow, very painful jigsaw puzzle, I have managed to work out the sequence of events. Yes, I know *what* happened now, but I will never know *why*. Who will ever be able to say what goes through the mind of a killer?

It could have destroyed me; I know that now. All of the trauma, pain and upheaval through the years, it could have ended very badly. The adults knew this – they kept a careful eye on me as a child. I was sent to a psychiatrist for regular check-ups. But it turned out I was pretty resilient. And I think I know the reason: it's because I remember everything. Maybe not the whole story, but I know what happened to Mum and me on that day. I remember it all so clearly and nothing can destroy or change those memories. It was the memories that made me strong and determined to live and to carry on, to get up each day and try a little harder. And now, thirty-six years later, I suppose you could say I got there. In the end I found my peace, my 'happily ever after'.

This book is for my mum, Susan Lowson.

You never got the chance of a 'happily ever after', Mum. Your life, hopes and dreams were taken from you and taken from me too. I know that if you were here today we would be as inseparable as we were when I was a little girl. And all those precious, special moments a mother and daughter should share through the years would be our memories together, our lives entwined as intimately as any mother and daughter. I know you wanted me to be happy. I know you wanted the best for me, so even when it was really hard, Mum, I carried on. I kept going; I did it for you.

Mum, I hope I made you proud. I love you. Forever.

Your daughter,
Amanda
December 2015

CHAPTER 1

THIS IS AFTER

Yes, that's me. A four-year-old girl in a hospital bed on a children's ward. I'm staring up at the ceiling, my face expressionless, giving nothing away, wondering how all this could have happened and where I'll end up now that my 'before' and 'after' story has begun.

This is after, but not like any after I have known like 'once upon a time' and 'happily ever after'. This is not a fairytale with a beautiful princess who marries a handsome prince and they live in a big castle happily ever after.

No, this is just plain after.

I shut my eyes tight and think to myself: this is a nightmare. It must be!

I want my mummy. I imagine her coming into the ward, running towards me, embracing me, telling me it's all been a bad dream, a nightmare. I feel numb and fearful of the future. I want to cry but I don't – I can't.

This is no nightmare – this is real. Oh my God, this is real! This is after.

CHAPTER 2

THE DAY
I DIED

Tick, tick, tick, tick... I watched the thin red second hand jerk round the clock face. From my bed at the end of the row, I could see straight into the nurse's station to the clock on the wall at the back. I watched it go round in a full circle until it reached the top again and a small flick of the minute hand signalled a whole minute had passed. *Tick, tick, tick, tick...* The second hand started on its long, slow journey once more and my eyes slid down to the matron at her desk, head down, brow furrowed in concentration as she filled in forms. She was short, this matron, with unruly brown curly hair, which looked like it wanted to escape from under her white cap. The phone rang, and she picked it up. I could barely hear her from my bed on the ward – she spoke briskly but quietly. They did everything quietly here, in hospital.

Nurses busied themselves on their rounds, moving here

and there, striding back and forth along the corridor, up and down the beds, along and back until they all blurred into one movement of blue and white. I closed my eyes for a moment. *They think I don't remember what happened, but I do. I don't think I'll ever forget.*

It all started with the clock, the clock at the side of my mother's bed...

Tick, tock, tick, tock, tick, tock... Brrrrrinnnnng!

The tiny silver hammer at the top of the wind-up clock flings itself against the two silver bells either side and the familiar loud noise pierces my dreams. At once I am awake, wide awake, staring at the familiar face of the clock, standing on its two feet and shaking like a little man, about to explode. Like on most mornings, I find myself curled up next to the warm sleeping body of my mother, Susan. Her honey-blonde hair is strewn across the pillow, her shoulders covered by her soft cream nightie and under the duvet her knees tucked up tight towards her chest. I have my own room at the back of our house in Stevenage, but since it is only the two of us living here, I often wander through to hers in the middle of the night.

But this morning is different from every other morning.

There is a man here, a strange man I have never seen before.

Brrriiinnng!

The hard, insistent alarm rings out in the bedroom and I am surprised to see the man here. He stands at the bottom of the bed and my eyes slowly adjust to the early-morning sunlight streaming through the curtains.

What is he doing? Pulling on his trousers, it looks like.

4

Getting dressed. Mum sleeps on next to me but I am wide awake and I watch as the man hops into one leg of his trousers then the other and pulls them up to his waist before buckling up his belt. He works quickly, urgently, as if in a rush...

Brrrrrrinnnnng!

Suddenly the man leaps towards my mother and grabs her. It happens so quickly. He takes her by the arm and drags her off the bed and now she is on the floor, fully awake, too shocked to scream. Her eyes are wide. In fear? Surprise? I can't tell – it is too quick.

Brrrrrinnnnng!

The man has my mum on the floor with both hands on her neck and he is pushing down hard so she can't breathe. Her mouth is open, like she is shouting, but her lips open and shut with no sound coming out. Then he smashes her head against the wall and her eyelids close. She is gone; I know that she is gone. She hasn't made a sound this whole time. Now he still has hold of her by the neck and he pushes down hard again. She seems to be changing colour – from pearly white to red and then purple.

A different noise fills the room.

It is me. Screaming.

'NO, NO, NO! STOP! PLEASE STOP! STOP HURTING MY MUMMY!'

I am crying, sat up on the bed crying and screaming for this man to stop hurting my mummy.

'Shut up!' he growls. His voice is low and hard. 'You better just shut up! Shut your bloody screaming or I won't stop!'

I want to stop crying, I really do. He says he will stop

5

hurting my mummy if I stop crying but it's really, really hard. I try to be quiet like he tells me but I'm very frightened and I know my mummy is really badly hurt. Now he drags Mummy from one side of the bedroom to the other and they are coming closer to me. I try to be quiet, but still he has his hands tight around my mummy's neck and her mouth hangs open, her eyes are shut, and I'm so scared I can't stop crying. He bashes her head against the wall again and then he gets up off her. He is coming for me...

I feel his strong hands around my neck now. He has pushed me back against the bed and I know what he is going to do. I feel myself sink back against the mattress and I know he is going to stop me breathing too. A pillow is placed over my face.

His hands are tight around my neck and the pain is getting harder to bear – I can't breathe.

It hurts too much.

I want this to be over now. I want it over.

Please just let it end...

I wake up again and I am on the bed still. I look over and here is Mummy. She's not on the floor anymore; she is next to me again. At the bottom of the bed there is a fire but I don't feel any heat from it – I don't feel anything at all.

Mummy looks peaceful – her mouth and eyes are closed – but I know I need to get her eyes open. I need to make her eyes open to make everything better.

Come on, Mummy. Wake up! Wake up, Mummy!

The man is gone and I am relieved that it is just the two of us again. I'm not scared anymore. It's all over now. I'm *with my mummy and if she opens her eyes it will all be okay. The alarm bell has stopped ringing and everything is peaceful and quiet. There is no pain, just the orange and yellow flames dancing at the bottom of the bed...*

It's okay. I'm with my mummy...

Now I am being carried down the stairs.

Who is this man? I don't recognise him. Another stranger. He carries me gently and we are moving down the stairs together. I look down at my legs and suddenly I notice the marks there and... oh! What is that on my foot? It looks like a giant bubble made of skin.

How did that get there?

We move out of the house and the cold outside air pierces my thin nightie and makes me shiver. The man carries me into another house. I know these people. They are my neighbours, nice people, kind people, with kind faces, but the voices are low and fearful. I am not worried now; I feel calm as the man places me gently down on the sofa. I breathe out and let my head fall back on the cushion...

Now there is a fireman talking to me. I know he is a fireman because I've seen the uniform before. The hard yellow hat with the badge on the front, the black coat with the shiny silver buttons and the bright yellow trousers. His chinstrap waggles as he speaks and I concentrate hard to hear him...

'Mandy, is it a small fire or a big fire?' he says. His voice is kind but urgent and I know I must try to answer.

'It's a big fire,' I say. I want to help him. He nods firmly and then he is gone.

7

My head falls back to the cushion. I'm so tired, I can't stay awake. I close my eyes.

I can't feel anything. Sounds and voices fade in and out, everything seems to be happening far away from me, as if I am still in a dream...

'Amanda?' the nurse stood at my bedside, a kind smile on her face.

'Mmmmm?' I answered groggily. How long had she been standing there?

'You have some new visitors today, Mandy,' she went on. 'These detectives have come to speak to you. They need your help. Is that okay?'

I nodded, still too dozy to speak. I liked this nurse. She was one of the younger ones, tall with blonde hair pinned up in a bun behind her head. She was the one I watched a lot from my bed next to the corridor. It was usually her that brought me my bedpan when I needed the toilet, and she was often the one doing the rounds with our food. I couldn't leave my bed because my legs were all bandaged up, from my feet right up to the top of my thighs. It was the fire, the doctors explained, when I was first brought here to Lister Hospital. The fire had burnt my legs and now I needed to stay in hospital to make them better again.

So I was stuck here, day in, day out. All the time. All the days and hours and minutes and seconds. *Tick, tick, tick, tick...* If I had to go to the toilet, they gave me a bedpan and if I needed to go anywhere else, they put me in a wheelchair. There were operations, there were mealtimes and there were visits from my family, but that was it. Every day I woke up in the same place: this bed in this ward in this hospital, not my mummy's bedroom. And though the ward was filled with other children and some nice colourful pictures of Winnie the Pooh, Piglet, Eeyore and Tigger on the walls, it wasn't like being at home. It was very, very different. My bed overflowed with cuddly toys, presents from my family to make me feel better. But there was nothing here from my home, nothing from before the fire. And no Mummy. It was like everything before was gone. And now life was different.

A smartly dressed man came towards my bed, followed by a woman in a navy suit, making loud, clattering sounds as she dragged two plastic chairs behind her.

'Hello, Amanda,' said the lady, plonking down the chairs in front of my bed. She wore thick make-up and a serious smile. 'I'm a detective with the police.'

There was a pause then as she looked at me for a reaction. I didn't move.

'Do you know what the police do, Amanda?'

I nodded and spoke in a small voice to the small brown teddy in my lap: 'Help people?'

'That's right, Amanda. We help people and we help to catch bad people who do bad things. My name is Sandra. Do you think you would like to try and help me catch that bad man who started the fire?'

'Yes.'

'Okay,' she said, taking out a big, black file from her bag and putting it onto the bed in front of me. The man sat down next to her.

'Oh, this is Ben,' she gestured towards the man. He had neat black hair and held a pencil and notebook on his lap. 'Ben is also a police detective and he's going to write things down on his notepad. That okay with you?'

My head bobbed up and down again. I liked the look of his notebook – it was very small and fitted into one of his hands. The pages flicked over the top of the pad instead of side to side like my own notebooks. I liked the way he flicked the pages over the top, I wanted to try it myself.

'We've got some pictures here, some pictures of men,' Sandra said as she heaved the file open in the middle. Inside were lots and lots of plastic folders, each one with little pockets holding pictures of men's faces.

'We hope that one of them might be a photo of the man who came into your house and made the fire. We really need your help here because we don't know which one it is. Do you think you could try and show us which one it might be?'

I nodded again as I watched Sandra flip through the plastic pages, searching for the right pictures. She had painted red nails and lots of gold rings on her fingers. I watched, entranced as her fingers snapped their way through the pages, red and gold flashing in front of my eyes.

Now Sandra flicked open the lever to take out a plastic folder with four pictures of different men in them. The faces all looked very serious, angry even, but I knew straight away none was the bad man who made the fire in my house.

'Now I want you to take your time, Amanda. I want you to look very carefully at these pictures I'm going to show you and you just let us know if you think you see one that matches the face of the man who came and made the fire. Is that okay? Do you think you can do that for us?'

I nodded again – I very much wanted to help this nice lady, Sandra. I knew that if I helped her, she might be able to catch the bad man. But he wasn't here. Not in the first set of pictures. After a few minutes of looking silently at the photos, Sandra asked me if I saw the man who did it and I shook my head.

'Okay,' she said, taking away the plastic folder and opening up her file again. 'Let's have a look at another set then...'

But he wasn't in the second set of pictures either. Or the third. Or the fourth. On and on it went. More pictures, more angry faces.

Sandra's red-tipped fingers pointed at each man's face.

'Not this one? No. This one? No...'

I felt myself tiring but I was determined not to give up. All the while, I tried to keep hold of the picture of the man's face as I remembered it from the morning he attacked me and my mum.

'Is that him?'

'No.'

'What about this one? Is that him?'

'No.'

'This one?'

'No.'

'What about him?'

That night I fell back into bed, exhausted from the effort of trying to help the police, but none of the faces had fitted the picture in my mind and when Sandra and Ben left, I felt bad: I wanted to help them. I hugged my teddy tightly. I really, really wanted them to find the man. I knew what he looked like; I remembered it all. The funny thing was they hadn't asked me about any of the other stuff, like what had happened to me that morning. Like what he had actually done. This confused me.

Why didn't they ask me what he did? Why didn't they ask me that?

That night, as the nurses moved swiftly but silently from bed to bed on their rounds, it occurred to me...

They think I don't know, they think I don't remember.

But I do.

I remember it all.

CHAPTER 3

CHICKEN AND CHIPS

'Okay, are you ready, Amanda?' the doctor asked, his words slightly muffled through the surgical mask. I nodded but felt scared at the same time. I could see that on his lap was a very large needle and I knew just what he was going to do with it. I sighed. Today was operation day. I lay on my back in the operating theatre, staring at the collection of cartoon animals parading across the ceiling. I imagined they had painted those animals up there to make kids like me feel better, but looking at the laughing bear in the red tutu holding hands with the grey horse and long-necked giraffe didn't make me feel better at all, not at all.

'Just remember, Mandy, it's chicken and chips after this!' the young nurse with the bun said. She stood just behind the doctor with the mask on, the one holding the very large needle. Her voice was uncomfortably chirpy.

13

Chicken and chips!

They always said this – I think they thought it would make me feel better. I shouldn't be scared or worried, they said, about the skin-graft operations because afterwards I would get my favourite meal, chicken and chips.

It was strange – I didn't know where they had got the idea the this was my favourite food. I mean, I liked chicken just fine and the roasted drumstick they served up after I came round from the surgery was nice and juicy. But chips? They were okay, I suppose. I wouldn't call them my *favourite*.

Perhaps, I thought as I lay waiting for the doctor with the long needle to put it into the back of my hand, perhaps they thought I loved chicken and chips because the very first time I had to have an operation I couldn't eat for the whole day before. So by the time they put a plate of food in front of me I was so hungry, I polished off the lot. My nan had explained to me that these were very new operations, very advanced *tek-nol-o-gee* she said, which meant that the doctors in the Lister Hospital in Stevenage didn't even know *how* to do them right. A very important surgeon had to come all the way from London to do them. Skin grafts – that's what they were called. I think she was trying to reassure me, but it didn't make me feel reassured at all. Not a bit of it. If anything, it made me more scared. *What if the doctor got it wrong?* I mean, if he hasn't done this before many times, how does he know he's doing it right?

But I didn't have much choice in the matter. I was stuck in hospital while they did these grafts on my legs. Even though I hadn't felt any pain from the fire, it turned out that a lot of skin on my feet and lower legs had been burnt away. That was the bubble I'd seen on my foot on the way down the stairs of the house. So the surgeons were taking little pieces of skin, or 'grafts', from my thighs to replace the skin that had been burnt off on my feet and shins. It sounded strange and I hated having to have the operations, but it wasn't up to me. It was the best treatment on offer, the doctors said, and I think this meant I should feel pleased that I was getting it. So every Thursday I was lured back into the operating theatre with the promise of chicken and chips.

Now the room swarmed with nurses and doctors, all busying themselves with their instruments and machines. I turned to look again at the doctor sat next to me with the big needle. I watched, fascinated and terrified at the same time, as he held the needle up in the air and tapped it twice with his knuckle. Then he exchanged a look with another doctor in a mask and they both nodded once very quickly.

'Okay, Amanda,' he said as he turned back to me, positioning the needle in the back of my hand. 'When you're ready, you can start to count to ten.'

I took a deep breath and stared at the laughing bear on the ceiling. *Ouch!* I felt a sharp sting as the tip of the needle pierced my skin, then a funny pulling sensation in my hand. *Why on earth was that bear wearing a red tutu?*

'One, two, three, four…'

'*Owwww!*'

I yelped as the two nurses lifted me gently back onto my bed on the ward. My legs really hurt now. I'd come round in the recovery room a little while earlier, feeling groggy and sick as usual. This was always the worst part, the bit after the operations when I felt dazed and in pain. The nurse in the recovery room usually gave me a sip of water then checked me over before sending me back to the ward.

Today my legs felt more tender than normal.

'Careful... Careful,' a short male nurse whispered to the nurse on the other side of me as they slid me onto my bed. 'Okay... one, two, three and slide.'

Ooooof! That time it really, really hurt. I looked down at my legs, bandaged right up to the thigh, just like before, only these dressings were clean, new and pretty tight.

'Are you okay, Amanda?' the male nurse asked. He had floppy dark hair and his upper lip shimmered with tiny beads of sweat.

'I'm fine,' I said quickly. 'It just hurt when you moved me. I'm fine now.'

I smiled at him and he grinned back, relief relaxing his features. Then he wiped his lip with the back of his sleeve and the pair of them left, swinging the trolley back down the corridor.

It wasn't long before the orderly came round with lunch and the promised plate of chicken and chips arrived on my tray. I smiled weakly as she filled up my water cup but in truth I didn't feel very hungry. *This was my favourite, wasn't it?* That's what all the doctors and nurses all thought and I didn't want to disappoint them, so I did my best to eat some. But really, the smell of the deep-fried chips sent little waves of nausea up and down my throat.

'Is my nan coming today?' I asked the matron when she came to check on me after lunch.

'Yes, I think so…' she murmured, flipping over the upside-down watch pinned to her uniform and writing something on my chart.

'Which one?'

'Which one?' she repeated, still writing, her brows knitted together in confusion.

'Yeah, which Nan is it? My Nan Eve or my Nan Floss?'

'Erm… erm… I, er, I don't know, Amanda. I'll go and check for you.' And with that, she bustled off to the nurse's station to consult the visitors' roster.

Nan Eve was my dad's mum. Her and my Grandad Frank lived in a nice big house on a street called The Paddocks and my dad lived with them. Once, my dad had lived with Mum and me in Colestrete, but that was ages and ages ago. Until *the dreadful thing* I hadn't seen him much except when I visited Nan Eve and Grandad Frank at The Paddocks, so I didn't really know him very well. His mum, my Nan Eve, was quite short and rounded, and she had dark olive skin with dark, curly brown hair and brown eyes. She looked exotic, as if she came from a foreign country, and was always smartly dressed in neat dark dresses. My Grandad Frank was slim and tall, with grey hair, and wore a shirt and a tie, as though he was always off to work.

I suppose I was closest to my Nan Floss and Grandad Bill. Before the fire, my Nan Floss had come round to our house a lot and she and my mum were close. Floss was very lovely and kind, and I loved her very much. They also brought a lot of presents for me while I was here.

'It's your Nan Floss and Grandad Bill,' the matron called out from the doorway of the nurse's station. 'They won't be long, Amanda.'

I nodded and looked at the clock again on the nurse's station wall. Time was a funny thing in hospital. Sometimes, it went so slowly, it was painful. At other times, it moved before you even had a chance to think and then, suddenly, it was nighttime before you'd even woken up properly. I picked up the workbook I had been writing in that morning before my operation and flicked through the pages I'd already written on. Line after line of patterns, drawn with a careful and steady hand, little swirls going up to the diagonal and then down again. Up, swirl at the top, and then down again.

This was the work we were set in the ward – it wasn't difficult but I suppose it helped pass the time. I had met a few of the children here, but it was difficult to make friends when I couldn't get out of bed. Occasionally, if one of us got a new toy, we passed it round to the other children so everybody could have a go holding it and playing with it. But I didn't always like doing this. Last week my Grandad Frank had brought me in an electronic game called Simon, which had four big buttons on it, each one a different colour: red, yellow, blue and green. When you switched Simon on, the computer inside made the buttons light up in a different order each time and you had to copy the order, just like the game 'Simon Says'. The pattern of the colours got harder each time, so you had to concentrate really hard not to make a mistake. It was a really brilliant gift because I could just play it on my own in my bed and it never got boring.

I was on it for ages and really enjoying it, but then the nurses said some of the other children wanted a go and so reluctantly I agreed for them to pass it round. The first two girls weren't really interested but then it got passed to a boy called Kevin, who was a bit rough. At first he found he could follow the right order but as the game got more difficult, he grew angry and careless and even dropped Simon on the floor once. I gasped and my whole upper body locked with anxiety. *What if he breaks it? What if he breaks my special present from my grandad?* I wanted so much to run over there at that minute and grab Simon off him. But I couldn't. I couldn't even get out of bed. *He doesn't care!* I fumed. *He doesn't care because it's not his game!*

Eventually, I became so frightened for Simon, I called out to the nurses: 'Please bring Simon back now. I want it back now.'

Ashley, an older nurse, brought the game back to me, looking perplexed.

'Now, why would you want to take it back so quickly?' she asked. Ashley had a strange accent that reminded me of rainy days by the sea. Everything she said sounded like a song. She told me once it was because she was *Eye-rish*.

'I don't want him to break it,' I whispered. 'He's dropped it twice now and it was a present from my grandpa.'

'Hmmm. Okay,' she nodded. 'That's understandable then. It's a very good game you've got there and you've to be keeping it safe now.'

Up, swirl, down, swirl, up, swirl, down, swirl...

My hand drew the patterns as my mind wandered back to that nerve-shredding day with my new present last week. It was so easy-peasy, this. Why did the teacher make us do this all the time? I wanted to do other stuff, but these patterns, this was the only work I was given to do in hospital. Before the fire I was learning my ABCs and sums in school. It was fun – in fact, I wanted to do some more reading and sums now but all I had were these stupid patterns. *Hummph! I could do these patterns with my eyes closed. Hey, that's an idea! I'll do them with my eyes closed.* So I did. Eyes tight shut, I let my pencil move in the same way it had done just a moment before.

Up, swirl, down, swirl, up, swirl, down, swirl, up, swirl, down, swirl, up...

'Amanda!' Nan Floss's voice was so close to my ear I jolted in surprise. I must have started to fall asleep just then.

'Nan!' I grinned and I let my Nan Floss envelop me in a warm, bosomy hug. Grandad Bill stood behind her, an awkward grin playing over his creased face. 'What about a cuddle for your grandad, then?'

'Grandad!' He leaned over the bed and patted me on the back. It was so good to see them both, such a relief. These were people I knew! People who loved me!

'I brought you something,' Grandad teased, his eyes twinkling.

'What is it?'

'It's a special present for my brave little girl,' he said.

'What?' I played along.

'See if you can guess...'

'Oh, just give it to her!' Floss nudged my grandad but she could see we were both enjoying this little game.

'Is it a teddy bear?' I asked.

'Close… but not quite. Try again.'

'Is it a bunny?'

'Nope.'

'A cat?'

'No.'

Suddenly, I felt a surge of excitement: 'Oh, is it my Nellie from home?'

I had an old blue elephant teddy at my home in Colestrete and I really hoped it was her. I loved Nellie so much – in the 'before' world, she had slept with me every night.

'No. Sorry, Amanda, love, it's not your Nellie.' Grandad looked downcast and suddenly Nan Floss erupted, sounding very cross.

'Oh, for God's sake, Bill, just give her the sheep!' she muttered.

'It's a sheep!' he said faintly, now looking really sad, and pulling out a fluffy white lamb, with little black hooves and black ears, from behind his back.

'Oh, it's lovely!' I said, trying hard to sound excited. I didn't want him to be sad like this and so I grabbed the lamb and hugged it into me, covering it with kisses. But really, I just wanted Nellie. I wanted something from my old life, anything!

Nothing had come out of that house except me. It was as if all the things I had had before were gone – my mum, my house, my clothes, my toys. There was nothing, nothing left at all. At that moment I felt very, very lonely.

Still, I kept that smile on my face. I didn't want my nan and grandad to feel any worse than they did already. Nan Floss perched herself at the edge of my bed, fanning out her navy skirt around her, and asked me all about the operation that morning. Grandad stood behind her, one hand on her shoulder and another behind his back. I told them about the needle and the doctor who made me count to ten but how I fell asleep before I got to 'ten'. And then I told them both about having chicken and chips for lunch. They said they were proud of me, I was a very brave girl and I just had to stay in hospital to get better. It wouldn't be too long now; I just had to be patient…

I know my mum is dead – I know it because I saw her die. Yesterday the social worker lady said that she was dead too. It was strange hearing her say it. I knew it was true because I watched my mummy die but even so… even so… I have this tiny little hope inside me that one day she might walk back in here. Like today, for instance, it feels like she could just walk back in and everything about the fire and the burns and the operations will disappear, all like a bad dream. I keep looking at the door, looking to see if she is standing behind it. Mum? Mummy? Are you there?

Too soon visiting time was over.

'Are my other nan and grandad coming tomorrow?' I asked Floss before she left.

My grandad was helping her into her brown coat and I could see that her body seemed to snap to attention, like a soldier, when I asked her that question.

'I honestly don't know, dear,' she replied, but the warmth had gone from her voice. She sounded tight and brittle. 'I don't know what your Lowson family are doing.'

It seemed like a funny thing to say but I didn't pay it much attention.

There was a lot of this sort of thing these days, I'd noticed – a lot of anger and tension. Everyone was so angry all the time and I knew it wouldn't do any good to ask them why so I just kissed my nan before she left and she softened as she held my face in her hands.

'Oh, Amanda,' she said, her eyes filling with tears. 'Amanda, we're so lucky to have you. Really, I don't know what I would have done if...'

'Now, come on, Flo.' My grandad was by her side, hand on her shoulder, thick, coarse fingers urging her away. 'Come on,' he repeated, a quiver in his voice, and Nan shook her head, kissed me once on the forehead and turned and left.

'We'll be back at the weekend,' Grandad smiled.

But I saw no happiness in that smile, just sadness – a lot of sadness.

Mostly, hospital was okay. Not too bad, not too good. The only thing I really hated was the baths. Every few days, I was wheeled into the bathroom where Gemma, the nurse with the bun, ran a bath with something in it that smelt like the operating theatre. I once asked her what it was and she told me it was *diss-in-fekt-ant*. It smelt like medical stuff, it smelled like operations, and it made my stomach turn – I hated that smell.

Gemma would help me get my nightie off and then gently put me into the bath with the help of a little swing that lowered me down into the water. I'd have to lie there for a while as the bandages soaked through and then, when it looked like they were really wet, she would very gently unravel them in the bath.

Urrggghh! It was horrible. *Horrible!*

Every time it was the same – the bandages always got stuck to the blood and the scars on my legs, so they pulled at my skin when we took them off and hurt really badly. And then, here, in my bloody, yucky-smelling bath, I got to finally see my legs. They looked awful. Up and down each one were great big scars and lots of mismatching skin, like a patchwork quilt that had been sewn together really badly. I hated it, hated every minute of it.

And as time wore on in the hospital, I became really fed up with the whole situation. I hated being stuck indoors all the time, stuck in my bed, unable to get up and walk around or even take myself to the toilet. I missed going outside, running around, just playing normally like I used to before the 'bad man' came. Even when they stopped giving me the bedpan and I was taken to the toilet in the wheelchair, it was annoying. The problem was they didn't just take me on my own; when we went to the loo there were usually four or five of us children and at least two nurses.

The nurses would natter, natter, natter while us children got on with our business. One afternoon, I'd had a wee and we were waiting around for ages for the others while the nurses chatted away as if they had all the time in the world. I was fed up, hanging around in this stupid toilet – I wanted to go back to the ward.

Eventually I spoke up: 'Can we go now, please?'

One of the nurses looked down at me from where she leant against the tiled wall. She was a new nurse, one I didn't know very well. She had a tight plait that ran all the way from her forehead to the back of her neck.

'No,' she said loudly. 'You need to stay and do a poo.'

I felt my face flush with embarrassment.

'But I don't need a poo,' I said in a little voice. 'I want to go. Can I go, please?'

'You've got to have a try,' she said. 'Go on, have a try. We're not going back to the ward until you do.'

So I sat on that cold, hard toilet seat for ages, my face hot with shame at being made to do a poo for this stupid nurse. Finally, I exploded: 'I DON'T WANT A POO! OKAY? I JUST WANT TO GO BACK TO THE WARD!'

I wanted to cry, but I didn't want to do it in front of everyone like this. I hated that nurse; hated her. I just wanted to go home now and for everything to go back to how it was before.

Happy Birthday to you.
Happy Birthday to you.
Happy Birthday, dear Amanda
Happy birthday to you!

The voices came from all over the ward as Gemma, my nurse with the bun, wheeled in a large white frosted cake on a trolley, my name picked out in pink swirly icing and five little wobbly candles on top. The cake was very big, bigger than any I had ever seen before, and all the doctors and nurses sang in very

25

loud voices, hands gesturing to the children to join in. Some did, others shouted the words, a couple slept through.

It was my fifth birthday, 20 April 1980. The *dreadful thing* had happened on 4 March, which meant I had already been in the hospital a very long time. Still, all the staff here tried to make this a special day for me. They gave me cards and presents and I was told lots of times that the hospital chef had made a cake especially for me, which was a really big thing because apparently he didn't do that for everyone.

So I knew I should feel very special.

Everyone was trying so hard.

I smiled back and blew really, really hard at the candles. I ate an extra-large slice of cake, which was vanilla sponge with jam and cream in the middle, and even asked for 'seconds'. Someone put a party hat on me, some of the children from the ward got out of bed and came to talk to me, and all through the afternoon, I tried my best to be happy. I tried really hard.

But underneath I felt empty and sad. It was my birthday and all I really wanted was my mum, to feel her holding me again.

CHAPTER 4

A VISIT

'Where are we going?' I asked Gemma as she eased me into the wheelchair.

'Just wait and see!' she replied. I had my back to her but even so, I could tell she was smiling as she spoke.

'Right, think we better get your dressing gown on,' she said, and she plucked my new pink dressing gown from the chair next to my bed. Everything was *new* these days. It wasn't like my old dressing gown – my old one was really soft from having been put through the washing machine so many times. This towelling dressing gown still felt hard and scratchy. She held out each arm and I slid them in, one at a time.

'Can you tie it yourself?' she asked, and I nodded. As soon as I had wrapped the dressing gown firmly around my middle, we set off.

At first, everything was normal. Gemma wheeled me out

of the ward and into the wide green corridor with the large pictures of fishing boats on the walls. We turned right and headed through a big set of double doors, wheels squeaking on the lino beneath me. But instead of turning left at the end as we usually did when we went to the canteen, we carried straight on, towards the lift.

'Where are we going?' I asked again.

'A surprise...' Gemma whispered, leaning down to speak close to my ear. We waited a short time for the lift and then, once inside, Gemma pressed the G button.

G?

G was the ground floor. G was the outside! I hadn't been outside since I came into the hospital. Suddenly my heart began to race and I felt a surge of excitement.

The lift juddered as it took off and slowly moved down through the different floors. A loud groaning noise signalled we had arrived at the ground floor and slowly the doors slid open.

Straight in front of me I could see a pair of large glass doors, sunlight streaming through so bright I could barely look. The doors opened and closed automatically as dozens of people went in and out of the hospital. I was mesmerised by all the different people. Some were visitors, arms laden with flowers and bags of grapes, faces set with worry. Others were hospital staff, busy-looking nurses and doctors, little plastic ID badges swinging from their necks, some holding folders and files to their chests, others clasping sandwiches or cups of coffee. A few patients in their hospital gowns hung around the front entrance, puffing miserably on cigarettes.

28

'Come on,' said Gemma, swinging me round to face the other way. 'It's on the other side.'

For a moment my heart sank – I longed to be out there in the world, to feel the sunshine on my face, to be among all the people, with all their busy lives. The ward was so silent, so boring compared to this; I felt so cut off from it all. But I had no time to think about that now. Gemma quickly spun me in the opposite direction and we began to roll down the ground-floor corridor towards the back of the hospital, passing all sorts of signs for different wards.

There were definitely more people here on the ground floor, and more interesting things to look at – we passed a shop selling sweets, magazines and teddy bears. I recognised one that had been given to me by my grandparents' neighbours. There was also a little café, where people sat at round blue plastic tables, drinking tea and talking quietly. We went through two more sets of double doors before Gemma turned left and suddenly, without any warning, we were outside. The cold, clean air struck me on the chest and I gasped. For the first time in months I felt the sun on my face.

It was a beautiful day. The sky was bright blue, bluer than I had ever seen it, and the air felt crisp and sharp.

'This is our hospital garden,' Gemma explained as she wheeled me down a little ramp and towards a small enclosed walled garden. Concrete paths circled well-kept plant beds overflowing with all kinds of different flowers and shrubs. Some I recognised, like the smooth purple cones – these were tulips – and the small yellow flowers with black 'faces' in the middle were called pansies, but others were a mystery to me. All I knew was that I loved the beautiful mess of colours and shapes.

In the centre of the garden stood a large grey stone fountain. Water bubbled up out of the top spire into a small basin underneath and then spilled over the sides into a bigger basin and so on until it reached the large basin at the bottom, which shimmered with silver and bronze coins thrown in by hopeful wish-makers. In each corner of the garden, there were thorny rose bushes surrounded by low hedges and then, along the back wall, on every side, there were wooden benches for people to sit on. This morning, there was nobody here, just us.

It felt like the first time I had ever been outside.

Each green leaf on each bush and plant popped out at me, so sharp and clear it was as if I could see each one individually. I could see all the tiny details, all the veins on the leaves and petals, as if I had special sight. The air was so clean and fresh; it was exhilarating and somewhere, from deep inside me, I felt a stirring. A sense of something I couldn't quite explain. But it was a nice feeling, a good feeling.

Gemma had been peering in and out of the bushes and suddenly she let out a little squeal of excitement and ran back over to me.

'It's over here,' she breathed, wheeling me in the direction of a low hedgerow, which was about the same height as me. Once we were right up against it, she pulled the wheelchair backwards to put on the brake and then leaned down next to me.

'In here,' she whispered, pointing into a thick, dense part of the hedge.

I followed the line of her finger and peered into the tangle of twigs, leaves and branches, looking deep inside to see what she was pointing at.

Suddenly, a movement caught my eye. A little flutter. *What was that? A wing?*

A bird?

As my eyes got used to the darkness inside the hedge, I could see a small but perfectly constructed bird's nest made of chestnut leaves, tiny twigs and feathers.

And there, perched on the edge of the nest was a plump brown bird.

'It's a sparrow,' Gemma whispered in my ear, so faintly I could barely hear.

The sparrow had a white neck, jet-black face, and front and feathers alternating brown, black and white down its back. It was breathtaking to see this delicate little bird, with its bright shiny eye and little black beak just resting there on top of this well-made, neat little nest.

And what was that noise? It sounded like squeaking. Now I could just make out tiny little beaks opening and closing in the nest. The sparrow bent down and put her own beak next to them. Suddenly, I realised this was a mummy bird feeding her new chicks.

My heart swelled as I watched the beautiful little scene. The mother sparrow, feeding each hungry chick in turn, hopped round the outside of the nest to get to them all. I turned back up to Gemma and smiled. This time the smile felt good, like it came from inside me.

'Thank you,' I said. And I meant it. For the first time in a very long while, I felt happy. We stayed watching the birds until the mother sparrow flew off out of the hedgerow, probably to get some more grubs for her little ones to eat.

'Come on,' urged Gemma. 'Better get you back in before the others start wondering where we've gone.'

But I didn't mind. I didn't mind going back inside now. *It's going to be okay*, I told myself and somehow I knew this was true. For the first time since the fire, since that man had tried to kill me, since I had lost my mum, I felt happy to be alive – it felt good.

I had hope again.

CHAPTER 5

NAN EVE AND NIVEA CREAM

*P*oint *and flex. Point and flex. Point and flex. Point and flex…* I said the words over and over again in my head as I sat on the carpet in my bedroom, watching as my toes pointed and then pulled back up in turn.

It was one of the exercises the *fizz-ee-oh* said I had to do to help my new skin grow properly around my feet. The *fizz-ee-oh* was a lady doctor, who would come onto the ward and show me how to do these exercises. But now that I was living with my Nan Eve and Grandad Frank, I had to remember to do them on my own. So every night, after my bath and after my Nan Eve had gently rubbed Nivea cream onto my legs to make them all soft, I sat on the floor like this and pointed and stretched. Sometimes I did it in the evening when I was watching TV, or when I was sitting at the table, waiting for my dinner. I did it whenever I remembered, and I knew it was

33

important so that my new skin didn't start to feel tight around my toes and feet and start to pull.

I felt a big relief the day I left the hospital to move into my Nan Eve and Grandad Frank's house at 54 The Paddocks. By now, I was out of the wheelchair and could walk a little on my own, though I still wore tight white stockings, like sock bandages, all the way up to the tops of my thighs. On that warm spring day at the end of April, Dad helped me up the stone steps towards the open front door. I still didn't know him very well because he hadn't lived with Mum and me in our 'Before' lives. Well, that wasn't quite true – my Nan Eve told me that Dad had lived with us until I was about two and then he went back to live at The Paddocks. Either way, I didn't remember it so, although I liked being with my dad, I didn't know him very well. Still, I was pleased to be returning somewhere familiar, somewhere from my past, though I wondered about my old house.

'You can't live at your old house because of the fire,' Nan Eve had explained one day when I asked her about it. 'So you're going to come and live with me, your grandad and your dad. Is that okay?'

I'd nodded, grateful that someone had explained what was happening. Until then, I'd had no idea where I was going to live or with whom. In the 'Before' world it was all so simple, so routine, I didn't even think about where I was living. I had Mummy, and that was that. I barely thought about what would happen the next day or the day after. In the 'After' world, it was different. Now I was worried about the future, about where I would end up and who would look after me. I couldn't help worrying. What happened if the Bad Man took away my Nan Eve and Grandad Frank? Who would look after me then? Would it be Nan Floss and Grandad Bill? Or maybe Dad? Where would we live if we didn't live at The Paddocks? I tried not to think about it too much, but at night, when I couldn't sleep, the questions went round and round in my head.

My nan and grandad's house was neat and tidy, and the big lounge and dining area were connected by a brown carpet with orange squares on it. A large wooden table with barley twist legs took up most of the dining room and heavy matching chairs stood to attention around the table. Warm, delicious cooking smells came from the kitchen at the back, where Nan Eve spent a lot of her time. It led to a big garden outside, where I loved to play. At the very back of the garden, stone steps led down to a large grass field, which all the Paddocks' houses could use. Upstairs, there was the bathroom, a separate toilet, two big bedrooms belonging to my grandparents and my dad at the front of the house, and then my small bedroom at the back. It was lovely to have a real room of my own again, a place with four walls and a door I could close behind me. The problem with living on a hospital ward is that everybody is there all the time so you don't get any space of your own. My room here was decorated with pretty pink wallpaper, a border of yellow flowers, matching yellow curtains and white wooden furniture. The only exception was a large brown wooden wardrobe, where Nan stored her winter coats and 'good' dresses in plastic.

Nan's house ran to a dependable routine, almost as clockwork as the one at the hospital. Every morning, she would get up and dress herself before coming into my room to wake me up. Sleepily, I'd put on my dressing gown and my cheerful blue slippers with the fluffy pom-poms on the top before following her downstairs for breakfast, where I'd sit at the table, waiting to hear the familiar click of the kettle. Breakfast was usually toast and marmalade, soft boiled eggs (my favourite) and, very occasionally, kippers. But she didn't make kippers that often because the strong fishy smell stank the house out for hours. Dad usually ate a little before us because he started work early at his job as an engineer, but he always said goodbye and gave me a peck on the cheek before he left.

Lunch was usually something simple, like a white bloomer sandwich made with leftover meat from dinner the night before, but in the evening Nan always made a proper meal such as roasted chicken, lamb or grilled chops, boiled or mashed potatoes and a selection of fresh boiled vegetables. The table was always laid with the cutlery in the proper place, a side plate and napkin folded on top. My dad was usually home for dinner, so it was nice for all of us to be together.

I needed this routine; I needed this sense that everything was the same as the day before. After so much 'strangeness' in my life, it was comforting that I could wake up every day and feel I knew what was coming next. In the evenings I snuggled up next to my nan on the big brown leather sofa, sinking into the soft felt cushions as we watched TV together. Sometimes we were joined by her tabby cat, Tammy, who would sit on my lap while I stroked her. Curled up into Nan's warm body, I could almost feel normal again. For a few hours each night,

I forgot that I had bandages on my legs, that my home was destroyed and that my mum was dead. I was just ordinary Amanda, a normal five-year-old having a cuddle with my nan.

Only later, after I'd brushed my teeth, washed my face and got into bed, would the fear creep back over my body.

'No, don't turn the light off, please!' I begged Nan each night as she tucked me up before reaching over to switch off my bedside lamp. Nan was soft and understanding – she never wanted me to feel unhappy or scared.

'Alright, we'll keep this little light on then,' she agreed, with a concerned smile.

'Are you sure you can get to sleep like this?'

I nodded.

'I don't like the dark,' I said.

'Hmmm…' Nan frowned before kissing me on the forehead.

'Goodnight, sweetheart. Sleep tight.'

Then gently, she'd tiptoe out of the room and close the door carefully behind her, as if not to disturb my journey towards sleep. But I knew that sleep would take a long time to come. Alone in the bedroom at night, I felt trapped, unable to breathe and really, really scared. At first I didn't even know what I was scared of. It was only later that I began to hear *the voice*.

We didn't talk about Mum much. In fact, it felt like my family was frightened to mention her in front of me, though I was desperate to talk about her, to remember her and bring her back to life with my words. She was with me still, somewhere inside my head and my body; I could still feel the warm touch of her skin, the silky texture of her hair, and hear the gentle rise and fall of her voice. She was here but not here. Somewhere inside me, the sensation of being near to her was always just a fraction below the surface. I clung to those memories; I didn't want to ever forget. Sometimes I sensed her so close to me I felt I could reach out and touch her.

But if I brought up my mum to Nan Eve she'd sigh and smile at me sadly.

'Your mum's in a better place now,' she'd say, shaking her head. 'She's at peace, she's happy now.'

I would frown, confused.

I mean, I hoped it was true. Yes, I truly hoped that she was happy – but was it possible? How could she be happy if she wasn't with me? Is this what she wanted for me, for either of us? I couldn't quite believe that my mum was happier now – in Heaven, wherever that was – than she was before, and I didn't really understand why Nan Eve said that. What did she mean? I wanted to ask her to explain but at the same time it felt like I wasn't meant to. The way they said these things, it was like that was meant to be the end of the conversation. So I shut up.

What I wanted more than anything was to speak to Nan Floss about my mum, but neither she nor Grandad Bill came to visit us at all. It was as if they had disappeared. One night, when I asked my nan and grandad about this over dinner, there was a heavy, dark silence and then Grandad looked down at his plate and coughed.

'Good chops, these,' he said, gesturing with his fork at his half-finished lamb chop.

'Yeah, they're really nice, Mum,' Dad echoed.

Silence again. *What did this mean?*

It was as if they didn't hear me, or they didn't *want* to hear me. It wasn't just Nan Floss and Grandad Bill, either. I didn't see any of my mum's side of the family at all these days. My mum's sister Carol and her husband Mick and their two kids used to visit me in hospital. So did my Uncles Kevin and Keith. They had all come while I was on the ward in hospital, but now that I was here, they didn't come at all. I looked around the table, hoping somebody would explain, but nobody caught my eye.

A minute later, Nan clapped her hands and asked brightly: 'Right, who's for pudding?'

It was so confusing. In this new 'After' world there was so much that didn't make sense to me, so I learned to avoid bringing up difficult subjects that made everyone go silent or get twitchy and irritated. Mum was one, my mum's side of the family was the other, and the fire was the third. And not because they wouldn't talk about it, or because they said things that made me confused – just because they got it wrong.

'You were in your bedroom,' Nan Eve told me one night as she spread thick, cool dollops of Nivea on my legs. 'That's where you were when the fire started.'

I stared at her blankly, not saying a word.

'In your bedroom,' she said again, smoothing the silky-white cream over the bumpy scars on my shins. 'And that's when it happened. That *dreadful thing* happened to your mum in her bedroom.'

This was totally wrong. I had been in my mum's bed when

39

the fire started – I had watched her die in front of me. But I didn't want to say anything. Nan and Grandad, they had their own ideas and I didn't want to tell them they were wrong. It felt too hard. I didn't want to upset my nan. I didn't want to upset myself by remembering. It was too much and right now, all I wanted was the comfort and love of my grandparents. *What does it matter now anyway?* I told myself. *It's over. It doesn't matter what anybody thinks.*

For the first few weeks, life at The Paddocks was very quiet. Nan occasionally took me on little walks to the park, or we caught an early bus into town to go for breakfast at Littlewoods, and of course there were many hospital check-ups. In the afternoons, after our trips, we'd return to The Paddocks, where Nan cut up fruit for me and put on some music in the living room while I did some colouring-in, or I played outside in the garden. I loved to be outside. More than anything else, I just wanted to spend time in the garden, playing on the swings or bouncing around on my space hopper. Out in the fresh air, I felt free and happy. Dad took me out at the weekends – usually to the park – this was nice because I didn't remember us spending time on our own together before the fire. It felt good to be around my dad – he was really young and he liked to laugh and joke around a lot. Occasionally, on Sundays, Dad's older brother Norman came to lunch with his wife Lorraine and two children, Daryl and Christina. Out came the good crockery, the white bone china tureens for the vegetables and the special gravy jug, which everyone called a 'boat'. I enjoyed it when Daryl and Christina visited – just four and three, they were gentle, friendly souls. My dad's older sister Carolyn didn't visit often as she lived in Slough.

One Sunday, Dad explained to me that he was youngest of his siblings. 'The accident!' Grandad interrupted and everyone round the table laughed, though I didn't understand the joke. There was three years between all of them, Dad went on, and Carolyn was the eldest. I wished I had a younger brother or sister at that moment, someone I could play with. Life at home with my grandparents was nice, but very quiet.

Suddenly, something occurred to me.

'Didn't you like living with my mum, then?' I asked Dad. It seemed to me that she would have been sad and a bit lonely without my dad there.

Another strained silence. The air in the room became thick and unbreathable.

'Things… things… erm didn't really work out between your mum and me,' he said after a while, though it looked like it hurt him to say it. 'I tried. Really, I did, but it was just too hard.' And he left it at that.

As time went on, my legs got a little better and in September Nan and Grandad bought me a new school uniform so I could start going to the primary school near them in Shephall. I had been at a different school before *the dreadful thing* had happened, but it was a school near my house in Colestrete and now, I didn't live there.

'You don't need to be worried or nervous,' Nan reassured me as she braided my long honey-coloured hair into two plaits on the morning of my first day of school. 'Everyone will be very kind and I'm sure you'll make some good friends.'

Actually, I wasn't worried at all – I couldn't wait!

It had felt like a long time since I'd played with other children my age and I was really looking forward to doing normal kid things again, like painting, learning my ABCs and playing outside. I had made a few friends in my old school but it had been so long since I'd been there I'd forgotten their names and what they looked like, so I was ready to meet some new children. The only thing that worried me was what to say about my legs.

'What if the other children ask me about the burns?' I asked Nan. I didn't want to explain what happened to everyone; it felt too painful.

'If anyone asks, just tell them it was an accident; a pan of boiling water fell on your legs,' she said. 'Then you don't have to go into all the stuff about the fire.'

That seemed like a good idea.

I bounced along by my nan's side that morning, swinging my brown satchel by my side, feeling the itch of the new clothes against my skin. My new uniform was very smart: a navy skirt, light blue shirt and black patent leather shoes. As we approached the school gates, I felt my heart pound with excitement. This was it – my new school! We walked through the big wrought-iron gates and into the playground of Peartree Infant School, where everyone seemed to be milling about, just waiting for something to happen. I looked around me – older kids raced up and down the length of the playground, playing a game of catch while a huddle of older girls stood to the side, chatting loudly. In another corner there was an energetic game of hopscotch in progress. It was noisy, boisterous and chaotic – and I loved it!

Suddenly, the air was disturbed by the loud clanging of a hand-held bell, being rung by one of the older children. A man in a suit stepped forward: 'Right, line up, everyone! Our new pupils can go straight in with Mrs Cleave.'

As the rest of the classes arranged themselves into neat lines along the playground, the man in the suit gestured to a smiling lady standing next to him. This was obviously Mrs Cleave – she had a kind, puffy-cheeked face and looked smart in a green woollen dress with a black jacket over the top. Her silvery-blonde hair was pinned up at the sides of her head and a pair of tortoiseshell glasses dangled at her neck on a smart gold chain.

'Okay, Class 7,' she trilled, clapping her hands together. 'Follow me, please!' Then she turned on her heels and started to march inside.

Nan Eve leant down: 'That's you – that's your teacher. Are you okay?'

I nodded, grinning from ear to ear.

'Good girl.' Nan seemed relieved. She kissed me on both cheeks. 'Well, have a lovely day. I'll be here to collect you when you come out this afternoon. Off you go!'

I started to follow Mrs Cleave through the big green doors at the entrance to the school when I noticed the crying. And it made me stop.

All around me, little girls and boys were crying. Some clung desperately to their mums, some just snivelled and sniffed, while a couple openly bawled: 'Mummy! I don't want to go in. Mummy!'

One red-faced little boy was building up to a full-on tantrum, right there in the playground.

'NO!' he screamed, eyes screwed tight, arms flailing wildly as his mother tried desperately to bring him under control. 'NO, NO, NO!'

Embarrassed-looking mothers ushered tearful infants towards the doors, whispering reassuring words into their ears. Some were pleading with them while others, exercising a tougher approach, just marched them in, stony-faced. I found myself walking slowly, taking in these fretful exchanges between mother and child on either side of me. I don't know why but they made me feel strange and unsettled. It was only later that it hit me and I understood: *These children, they are all crying for their mummies. That will never happen to me again. I will never cry for my mummy because my mummy is gone.*

I settled into school easily and was happy there right from the start. I made good friends and loved nothing better than playing outside with them on the climbing frames or making up games together. But as the month wore on, the tension in my nan and grandad's house grew worse and worse. It was as if everybody was waiting for something very bad to happen and it put me on edge. I had no idea what was going on until one morning, during our usual walk to school, Nan blurted it all out.

'It's a very big day for you, Amanda,' she said, her brown patent heels clacking loudly on the pavement. I didn't know what she meant. Today was a normal day really, nothing special at all. Now I counted the clacks as we walked. *One, two, three, four…*

'Honestly!' she exclaimed, angrily. 'I don't know what your Chalkley family are playing at. I really don't! I mean, what are they doing? What do they think they're doing? You're going to end up in a care home at this rate!'

WHAT?

What's going on?

Suddenly she had my attention. My Chalkley family was my mother's family – that was their surname – but I had no idea what she meant by going into a care home. Wasn't I just going to live with her and Grandad Frank until I was all grown up? I didn't understand. And what did Nan Floss and Grandad Bill have to do with care homes? Suddenly, I fell forward a little as my feet tripped over themselves. It was as if the pavement had shifted, making me unsteady and unable to put one foot in front of the other without deep concentration. For a moment, I was silent as I focused on just trying to stay upright. The blood pounded in my ears; I felt light and unreal.

'Er... what... erm... what do you mean, Nan?' I said.

There was no covering it up now – she had to tell me.

'Well, it's a court date,' she huffed. 'Your father is going to court today against your Chalkley family. They are taking him to court! And we're going to find out if you'll end up in care or not. Sweetheart, I honestly don't know what's going to happen today.'

At this I saw that her eyes had begun to swim with tears. She was trying to keep it together but she was very upset and that made me feel even more frightened.

'If it doesn't go well, we might not be looking after you anymore, Amanda. I'm sorry, it's just the way it is, none of us

45

wanted this to happen. We just don't know what the judge is going to say.'

I felt numb as I walked through the gates of my school that morning. On the surface at least, I was normal, happy Amanda but underneath, I felt terrified. *What is going to happen to me?* I couldn't concentrate on my lessons that day and I didn't feel like playing tag or hopscotch in the playground. Instead I sat on my own in the corner, gnawing at my fingertips, the same questions swimming round and round in my head: *What's going to happen now? Who would come to collect me after school if Nan Eve wasn't there? Would I still see my dad, or my grandparents if they put me into care? Where was I going to live?*

All day long I worried and fretted until I felt sick and wretched with uncertainty. Once again, my whole life was up in the air and I had no idea what would happen next.

CHAPTER 6

MY CHALKLEY FAMILY

Nan was grinning at the school gates. That was how I knew I wasn't going into care. Still, I didn't feel reassured until I was at her side, hearing the actual words from her mouth.

'No, no, it's okay,' she smiled, her voice softer and more relaxed than that morning as she gave me a big hug. 'The judge was very sensible. He said you could keep living with us and your dad, but he made an order so that you have to go and see your Chalkley family every other weekend and during the holidays.'

I was so relieved – it felt like my stomach had been scrunched up into knots all day long. Now I listened carefully as Nan explained: 'He's made you a ward of court. He's put a plan in place so that your other family gets access rights. I mean, I think he saw sense. After all, what would be the point of moving you away from us? No, it wouldn't have been right and I think we all knew their case was weak. But it *was* very worrying. Look, your father's at home. He can tell you everything in more detail. Let's go home and see him, shall we?'

All the way home, I went over it in my mind, but I couldn't for the life of me work out why my dad and my Chalkley family had been so angry with each other. How had it got so bad that they had to go to court over me? They all wanted to see me so why couldn't they just share, like I was always told to do? Why couldn't they just *get on*? My feelings were all over the place! Of course I was relieved I wasn't going to live in a care home, but I also felt bad for my dad and nan, having to go through something that sounded really upsetting. And yet, I was also quite pleased my Chalkley family had wanted to see me so much, and quietly, secretly, I was looking forward to seeing them too! After all, they were my family and I loved them. Not that I could say that in front of my dad, Nan Eve and Grandad Frank, which was silly, really. Why didn't they like them? What had they done wrong? Oh, I was all mixed up and still, at the back of my mind, there was a niggling unease about the situation. Was it real? Was everything *really* okay? I couldn't quite shake off the fear that had me in its grip all day long.

When I got home, Dad sat me down and went over the details of the judge's order. It seemed very complicated. The first weekend I had to go and stay with my mum's sister Aunty Carol, her husband Uncle Mick and their two children, Greg and Claire, from Friday evening to Sunday evening. The following weekend, I would go to see them on Saturday daytime only. The weekend after, I could stay at home with Nan Eve and Grandad Frank; the weekend after that, I would go to Aunty Carol's from Friday to Sunday again. Then it was Sunday daytime only, miss another weekend and after that the pattern would repeat itself. By the time my dad had finished explaining our new arrangements, my head was swimming.

'And then in the summer holidays, you go and stay with them for two weeks,' he concluded, reading the last paragraph of the judge's order. For a minute, he just sat there, staring at the sheet of typed paper in his hands. It was strange seeing him home from work on a weekday like this. He was dressed very smartly in his best brown suit and had brushed his thick, curly black hair back from his face. Now he leaned forward with his elbow on his knees, staring at the order with a fixed expression, somewhere between anger and confusion.

Eventually he shook his head and puffed out his cheeks.

'Seems mad, but there you go,' he sighed. 'I was just trying to do the right thing. Social services thought it would be better if you got used to us here first. I just did what they told me.' I didn't know what he meant but at that moment, I didn't care. I walked over to Dad and put my arms around his neck.

'I love you, Dad,' I said. And at that, he smiled at me.

Four days later, I was sitting in the living room in my best clothes: a burgundy corduroy skirt, mustard yellow polo neck and matching tights. There were butterflies in my stomach.

'Are you sure I don't need to take my toothbrush?' I asked Nan for the third time that afternoon.

'No, no, no,' she shook her head, as she bustled in and out of the kitchen, fussing and fretting. 'They can give you all of that. They want to take you away from us? Well, they can give you a toothbrush while you're there! You're not taking anything from this house!'

She was so angry, I didn't dare argue. Still, it felt very strange going to my aunt and uncle's house for the weekend without taking a toothbrush or even a change of clothes. But my nan was adamant she wasn't going to pack anything for me so I had no choice but to go empty-handed.

I looked at the clock – *tick, tick, tick!* The second hand moved slowly round the bottom of the clock up towards the twelve. Now it was 5.29pm. Just one more minute to go and he'd be here...

Ding, dong!

'Right, that's him, then,' said Nan, her mouth set in a thin line, her nostrils flaring as she breathed hard. She nodded at Grandad, who went to open the door. I followed him into the corridor just as Nan enveloped me in a big hug before straightening up, retreating to the kitchen and closing the door behind her. Dad was up in his room – he'd already said goodbye to me earlier.

'I'd rather not be downstairs when Mick comes to get you,' he'd explained as he sat on his bed, holding my hands in his. 'I don't get on all that well with your uncle. It's for the best, trust me.'

I said it was fine, but as usual, I didn't understand. All

I knew was that after I came back from school at 3.30pm, everyone had been very tense and angry. Nan snapped at Grandad twice, which wasn't like her at all, and she'd spent an awfully long time in the kitchen, slamming the cupboards much louder than was necessary. It felt like a dark cloud had settled over our house and it was all because I was going to stay at my aunt and uncle's for the weekend. I couldn't help it – I loved living with Nan Eve, Grandad Frank and Dad, but the way everyone was acting today, it made me feel like I actually wanted to go!

Grandad Frank opened the door and there was Mick on the doorstep. A tall, strong-looking man, he wore a pair of stonewashed jeans with a red jumper and a pale blue sports jacket. The two men didn't say a word to each other; Mick just turned and walked back to his car.

'Okay, love?' Grandad turned to me. 'You can go with your Uncle Mick now.'

And he bent down and gave me a kiss.

'We'll see you on Sunday,' he went on as I quickly shrugged on my coat and followed Mick out the door. It was already beginning to get dark but I could see Mick's car at the end of the stone steps because he still had his lights on. When Mick reached the car, he held open the door for me.

I hurried down all the steps and then jumped in the back.

'Seat belt on,' said Mick, then he slammed the car door.

I reached around and pulled the seatbelt down around me and heard it clunk as it found its place in the buckle next to my leg.

'Right,' Mick opened the driver's side door and got in himself. 'Let's be off, shall we?'

I sat quietly in the back, my hands folded neatly on my lap, staring at the top of Mick's head. Half of his head was covered by hair; the other half was bald. It was a relief to be in the car and away from all the strange tension at my Nan's house. I looked at the window as we passed by all the houses and streets lit by the orange glow of street lamps. My aunt and uncle lived in Bedwell on the other side of Stevenage, near to where my nan lived and round the corner from my old house on Colestrete. It wasn't far, just ten minutes till we pulled up in front of their three-bedroom house and Mick turned off the engine. We hadn't spoken much in the car. He had asked me how I was enjoying my new school and whether my legs were feeling better. I had answered 'yes' to both questions. Now I was a little nervous but also excited as he led me down an alley round the side of the house and through a small outhouse. I remembered coming here before with my mum and the memory cheered me.

As we stood in the outhouse I could see the bright lights from the kitchen through the glass panel on the back door. The dim light shone out onto the outhouse where we were standing. Mick went ahead of me, pushing open the back door and stomping his feet on the mat at the same time.

'She's here!' he shouted into the house. 'Amanda's here!' All of a sudden my Aunty Carol appeared in the doorway.

'Amanda!' she rushed towards me and picked me up, spinning me round. Then she plonked me down in the kitchen and stood back to look me over.

'Oh my goodness, Amanda! Look at you! Don't you look lovely! And so much taller! I can't believe it. I can't believe how much you've grown in just two months! Where has the time gone?'

She had her hands to her mouth and was shaking her head in wonder. I couldn't help grinning back at her. It was so good to see her too! She was my mum's sister and until this moment, I didn't realise how much I'd missed her. Even though they were sisters, my Aunty Carol and Mum looked very different to each other. Whereas my mum was slight, with long pale blonde hair, my Aunty had short brown hair and was thicker around the middle. They wore different clothes too – Mum had always dressed very casually in jeans and T-shirts whereas Carol liked silky blouses and long, flowing skirts. She was older than Mum and it always felt like she was more grown-up too.

'KIDS!' Carol stuck her head through the doorway and yelled towards the front of the house. 'Come on, kids! Your cousin is here!'

Carol bent down now and looked at me intently.

'You know we wanted to come and see you before now,' she said quickly. 'We wanted to visit as soon as you got out of hospital but we had to go through the whole court thing. It's not what we wanted at all, none of it. I'm sorry we had to go through with it.'

All this was delivered at breakneck speed, so I barely had time to register what she was saying before my cousins Claire and Greg bustled into the kitchen.

Aunty Carol stood up as they walked in. Claire was two years older than me with long blonde hair and hazel green eyes. Greg was also blonde, five years older and a big boy already. They both smiled when they saw me.

'Hi Amanda!' Claire said excitedly. 'You know you're staying in my room tonight? Do you want to come and see where you're sleeping?'

'Yeah, okay,' I said, and with that she took me by the hand and led me through the dining area and living room to the hallway and up the stairs.

It felt nice to be with my Chalkley family again. I still didn't understand what happened that made it so difficult for them to see me, or why it all ended up in a courtroom with a judge making me a ward of court, but it didn't matter now. The important thing was I had my family back again. That night Claire lent me a nightie because I didn't have one of my own and I slept on a mattress on the floor in her room.

'It's just for now,' Aunty Carol explained. 'We'll get you your own bed in here. And some nighties too so you won't have to borrow Claire's.'

This was a relief – I was swamped in Claire's clothes!

The next morning, I awoke, slightly confused. *What was I doing on the floor? Where was my bed?* For a moment I couldn't work it out and then it all came flooding back. I looked at the clock on the wall – 7.30am – this was the time Nan Eve usually came into my room to take me down to breakfast. But the house was ghostly still and Claire slept soundly, wrapped up in her duvet with her back to me.

'Claire?' I whispered.

'Urghh…' she groaned.

'Claire, can I get up now?'

'No, go back to sleep!' she muttered irritably.

'I *can't*!' I said.

It was frustrating. Usually, I was up early with Nan Eve, but it seemed the Chalkleys enjoyed a lie-in on Saturday mornings. Later, over breakfast, Aunty Carol suggested I take a *Beano* comic to bed with me so if I woke up early on Sunday, I could just lie there and read until the rest of the family were ready to get up. I was fast learning that being a houseguest at Aunty's was not the same as living with Nan Eve and Grandad Frank!

Later, we visited my Nan Floss and Grandad Bill. I was so excited to see my nan, I could hardly wait to leave the house and spent the morning bouncing up and down on the sofa, desperate to get outside and get going. *Nan Floss! I'm going to see Nan Floss!* When she opened the door to Aunty Carol and me, I flung myself into her arms.

'Oh, my dear,' she laughed, 'you almost took the wind out of me! Stand back, stand back now. Let's take a look at you.'

There seemed to be a lot of this sort of thing going on – but I did as I was told and stepped back obediently.

'Oh, my,' she exclaimed, tears in her eyes, 'look at you, so pretty! Just like your mum.'

It was exactly what I needed to hear! For so long I'd been afraid of talking about my mum, afraid of upsetting someone. But here, Nan had just come right out and said it. It was as if here, with my Nan Floss, I could relax, knowing that she too missed my mum just as much as me. She led me indoors. Inside, the walls were covered with pictures of Mum through the years. There she was as a young girl, around my age, with her older sister Carol and brother Keith, and younger brother Kevin. Here, above the telephone stand, there was a picture of her as a teenager sat on her beloved white horse, Sherry. There was even a picture of Mum in her bathing costume on a beach somewhere, wet hair plastered to her head, a yellow-and-white towel wrapped around her shoulders and a face full of happiness.

Mum! Mummy!

I wanted to stand and stare at those pictures all day long. They gave me such joy. There were no pictures of my mum on the walls of Nan Eve and Grandad Frank's house, but here, in Nan Floss's home, they were everywhere. Mum was real! A real person who smiled for the camera, and rode horses and went swimming and had fun.

Aunty Carol left me with my Nan for lunch and it was lovely, just the two of us, catching up over a ham and pickle sandwich. Grandad Bill had seen me earlier but he went down the pub after a short while and then the two of us were alone, pleased to be in each other's company again after so long. There seemed to be a special connection between us and while I was with her, I felt calm and relaxed. Afterwards, the family picked me up and we all went to the Lakes in the afternoon. The Lakes is actually a series of large lakes linked together in a huge area called Fairlands Park. There is a large playground and even a café which serves wine for the adults. Before, when she was alive, I would come here with my mum a lot, and returning now made me think of the times we were here together, the times she pushed me on the swings or stood, holding my coat, grinning, as I hurtled down the slide, yelling to her: 'Watch me! Watch me, Mummy!' And now, if I stood really, really still, I could almost imagine she was here again, just waiting to come and take me by the hand...

'Are you okay, Amanda?' Carol asked as I stood still as a statue on the edge of the playground, letting the fantasy take hold. Normally, I would be the first person to throw myself into the playground, but not today. Today, I felt the delicate touch of the past and I was afraid that if I moved an inch, that feeling of being close to my mum again would disappear altogether.

'Hmmmm... yeah, I'm fine,' I said, not really knowing what I was saying.

'You can tell me if you like,' she said, bending down beside me, one hand on my shoulder. I knew what she meant but I didn't feel like talking at that moment – I just wanted to keep those special memories to myself. I didn't say a word. Instead, I stood there, warmed by the sense of my mother, close to me again.

A few minutes later, I was playing with the other children, swinging on the climbing frame, bouncing up and down in the seesaw and spinning round and round on the roundabout. In the hazy September sunshine, I ran and played and laughed and spun till I was exhausted. It felt good to be outside, to run around and forget everything, even for just a few minutes.

From that weekend onwards, we stuck rigidly to the timetable that the judge had drawn up for both families. Every other weekend I saw my Chalkley family and though it wasn't always easy to fit in with their routine or way of doing things, I was grateful that they were still a big part of my life. At the end of each visit, I would come home to Nan Eve and

Grandad Frank, dying to tell them all the things I'd been up to and give them all the 'news'. But the funny thing was, they never asked about my Chalkley family, so I didn't talk about them. It was the same on the other side: my Aunty Carol never asked me how my Nan Eve was or how my dad was getting on. The two families never spoke about each other at all!

The other regular visits in my life were my once-a-month trips to see the *sigh-kite-trist* lady. They had started very soon after *the dreadful thing* and at first they were fine. But I quickly got fed up with sitting in Dr Grosse's office for ages, answering her stupid questions, when I would much rather have gone to the playground with my dad. Or even better, to the pool!

'I don't want to go, Dad!' I huffed one day as we sat on the bus together. Dr Grosse didn't work in the hospital, like the other doctors, but had a large brown office in a building that was miles from our house. It always took ages to get there and we had to change buses twice. It's not that it was bad or horrible, going to see Dr Grosse, just uncomfortable and boring, *always* boring.

'Hello Amanda,' she greeted me quietly, formally. Dr Grosse spoke like she came from another country and she had dark curly hair and jet-black eyes. She dressed smartly, like a teacher, and wore a pair of square black-framed glasses, just like the Greek singer Nana Mouskouri.

'How are you feeling today, Amanda?' she asked me as I trudged into the elegant office with the cream carpet and soft, light brown sofas.

'Fine,' I sighed. Dad stayed outside in the waiting room, flicking through magazines. *Click!* The door closed behind me and then... *Clunk*. The key turned and the door was locked. She had started doing this ever since I had tried to escape. It wasn't a big deal – one day I just got fed up of her silly questions and decided to go back to Dad. So I got up and walked out, Dr Grosse calling after me: 'Where are you going, Amanda?'

Now, whenever I went to the door, I found it was locked.

There was a doll's house in one corner of Dr Grosse's office and for most of our sessions, she just sat and watched me while I played with the dolls in the house. Occasionally she would ask me in her soft voice what I was doing and who the dolls were, but not always. Mostly she just sat in her large black leather chair, legs crossed, a little notebook on her lap and a pen poised thoughtfully against her chin, quietly watching me. There was nothing difficult about being here; it was quite a nice, relaxed thing just to play with a doll's house on my own, but the way she looked at me made me feel uncomfortable. In truth, it felt pointless, boring. I would rather have been running around outside.

As the last of the autumn leaves left the trees and the sharp, cold winter set in, I got used to my new life and routine. Now, I enjoyed being a weekend guest at my aunty's house, and the cosy visits with my Nan Floss. I even got used to reading in bed on Saturday mornings while my Chalkley family had their long lie-ins! The only change to the routine came one weekend when Nan Eve announced that I couldn't go to my Aunty Carol's that weekend because of a funeral.

'I'm really sorry, Amanda,' she said gently. 'It's your

Grandad Bill, he died earlier this week – it was a sudden thing, a big shock to the family. One minute he was right as rain, the next lying in the back garden. They couldn't do anything for him. I'm so very sorry, love. I know you loved your grandad.'

Oh my God!

My grandad?

It just didn't feel real, or right. My poor Nan Floss! She had lost my mum and now my grandad too was dead. It wasn't fair on her. It wasn't fair on me either!

That night I lay in bed and wept hot, salty tears under my duvet. I wanted my mum. More than anything in the world, I just wanted Mum there with me, her warm body circling mine, comforting me, making all the pain go away.

Nothing made sense in my life.

Nothing stayed the same.

CHAPTER 7

HIS VOICE

*O*h, *please go away! Please stop!*
It must be the middle of the night – it is pitch black outside and the house is completely still. Except I can hear a voice, a loud male voice in my head, and it's angry and scary. But the voice can't be coming from the house, otherwise everyone would be awake. It is so loud! I want it to stop but I don't know how. I don't want to hear it; I don't want to hear what it is saying, so I try covering my ears with my hands, but still, the loud noise comes.

What's going on? What's happening?

I hurl myself under the duvet and jam my thumbs against my ears. My eyes are scrunched up tight, as if that will help to drown out the terrible sound. But no, nothing! His voice is a low, rumbling growl, like the steady roar of a river, and now it is getting closer and closer. No! I don't want to hear it. I don't want to hear it!

Now I am up and sitting on the edge of the bed, unsure what to do or where to go to escape this terrible noise. My heart is thumping wildly and I can hear the sound of my own rapid breathing. I look over to the other side of the room at the large oak wardrobe in the corner. It appears to be vibrating up and down, humming almost, moving so rapidly and coming towards me at the same time. Then it retreats back to the wall again. I stare, petrified, as the large wardrobe looms over me and then falls back, moving so quickly it almost seems to hum. And what is that coming out of the wall? The wall seems to be moving, changing shape, and I can see a form emerging from it, like that of a person. It is a person! A man is coming out of the wall and he is coming to get me! Oh, no! No, no! My whole bedroom is alive and moving.

I can't take it anymore. I can't stay here! I don't want to be stuck in the tiny bedroom. I bolt out of my room and onto the landing, where thankfully my Nan Eve has left a light on in the hallway. For a moment, the bright light floods my vision, washing away the man's voice. From here, I slip into Nan and Grandad's room. They are fast asleep. I run to the window now and look out at the streetlights and the black, shadowy movements of the tree branches as they sway in the cold December winds. Desperately, wildly, my eyes dart around, trying to take it all in at once. I need to see the realness of the world, to fix myself to a time and place. This is real, I tell myself. This is real! Across the street, there are the other houses, some still with lights peeking out from under heavy curtains. Down on the ground, there is the road, the fences and gardens with all their bushes and flowers, just silhouettes in the darkness. And up now… I look up to see the stars, like pinpricks in the inky night, twinkling at me. Looking at them, far away, I start to relax and my heart stops thudding like crazy in my ears. I blink hard. The distant stars blink back.

Look, I tell myself, it is normal. The street is normal; everything is normal out here. I let out a sigh of relief – there's nothing to be frightened of. Slowly, my breathing returns to normal and for a while I hang onto the windowsill, just looking out onto the quiet, empty street. There's no one there; there's no one there. Finally, I steel myself to give my nan's shoulder a little tap.

Wake up, Nan! Please, wake up…

'What are you doing here, love?' Nan asked, squinting up at me.

'I couldn't sleep, Nan. I got scared.'

'What? Again? Oh, you poor thing!'

It must have been midnight or even later but Nan didn't scold me. She just pulled aside the cover and took my hand to lead me out to the hallway.

As we walked, she whispered to me, so as not to wake Grandad: 'What is it that's frightening you, dear?'

'I don't know,' I said hesitantly, rubbing my eyes. 'I hear this voice in my head and it scares me so I have to come out here for the light.'

'That doesn't sound very nice at all – no, not at all. Okay, then,' she said, squeezing my small hand in both of hers. 'Let's go in your room together and make sure there's nothing in there which might be giving you bad dreams.'

As I munched my way through my Cornflakes the following morning, I thought about *the voice* in the night. It wasn't the first time I had run out into the corridor to escape it. Going to bed was so hard these days. Every night I dreaded my 8pm bedtime, knowing that often I would wake up hearing that horrible voice. It frightened me so much. But I didn't know what to do about it and it seemed the only thing that helped was getting out of my bedroom.

'You've really got to try and stay in bed, love,' Nan Eve now said to me as she spread Marmite on her toast.

'Hmmm... I know,' I murmured.

I didn't want to be like this! I didn't like it; I felt bad for making my family worry about me and for acting so strangely, but I didn't know how else to stop *the voice*! One night, Dad had found me, curled up on the bathmat in the bathroom. I wanted a light in my room but they said it was best to try and get used to sleeping in the dark. For a while my nan and grandad put a little glowing plug in my room, thinking that might help. But it didn't. Nothing helped, and I frequently woke up in the night, quivering with fear and dread.

A few weeks later, I was back at my Nan Floss's house but without Grandpa the place felt dark and sad. Nan was very upset. So was my Uncle Kevin, who was Nan and Grandad's youngest son. He was my uncle but actually he was still very young, just turned twenty, and he had been very close to his dad.

'I'm so sorry, Amanda,' Nan Floss cried the first time I saw her. 'You lost your grandad!' She took me into her arms and wept. Aunty Carol and Uncle Mick looked on, blank faces but blazing eyes, as though they were very, very angry. Now they rushed towards Nan and put their arms around her, to try and stop her crying but later, I heard Mick muttering to Aunty Carol: 'It's just not right, none of it.'

'I know, I know,' she whispered back. 'Let's not do this now, not here.'

Later, when we were alone, watching TV, Nan Floss started talking to me: 'He was only fifty-six, your grandad. It's no age. It was a heart attack, they said, but you know what I think? I think your grandad died of a broken heart. That's the truth of it. He couldn't cope, not after we lost your mum like that. We did our best, both of us... You know, we tried to carry on, keep going.'

She got up now and walked to the window, putting her hand up to the curtain. A bitter little laugh escaped her lips.

'"Go on holiday!" that's what the doctor said. "Go away to Malta, forget about everything. Make yourselves feel better."'

Nan gripped the curtain tightly now and the thick brown material bunched up against her white knuckles. I wasn't sure if she even knew I was there anymore. She seemed to be very, very far away.

'It was the worst time of my life. The worst time! We went away, just like they told us, but it didn't work. It was just the same as before, only now we both felt rotten, miles from home. Day after day we were like that, watching the waves, wondering what on earth we were doing there. What to say to each other?'

Nan chewed on her bottom lip, frowning into the distance. Then she shook her head.

'It was no good. We came home and everything felt very grey, very bleak – all the leaves gone from the trees, grey skies; grey thoughts. Bill wasn't himself, neither of us were. How could we be the same after... after what happened?'

Nan paused. I stayed perfectly still as I strained to listen to the silence. From here, I could just hear the faint ticking of the hallway clock. *Tick, tick, tick, tick...*

'Just before his birthday, that's when he died. I found him, outside by the back door, he was gasping for breath but there was nothing I could do, you see?'

Now Nan Floss looked directly at me, her green eyes filled with tears. 'The paramedics tried to revive him but he was gone before he even got to the hospital. Broken heart, the man died of a broken heart.'

I ran to her now and threw myself into her arms.

Poor Nan! Without Grandad she seemed very lost and alone. She still had Kevin living with her, but he was a young man with a job and friends, so he wasn't at home all that much. I think she must have missed having her husband by her side. Nan Floss talked to me a lot after Grandad died. She told me all about coming to Stevenage. She wasn't from Hertfordshire originally, she said. She came from a place called Newcastle, which was in the north of England. They were very poor when she was growing up, she explained. Her mother struggled to feed all her brothers and sisters and they just lived in the one room, which was cold all the time. They had fun, all the children, but life was hard and Nan didn't get on with her dad so when she was a young woman, she left Newcastle and moved to London in search of a better life. That's where she met my Grandad Bill, a Royal Navy man.

'Very handsome, he was, in his uniform,' she smiled, pressing down on the curls of her hair with a flat palm, one at a time. 'And he was a kind man. He liked to have fun – always laughing and joking. Of course, sometimes he liked to have too much fun. I had to pull him out of the pub on more than one occasion!' And with that, she laughed at the memory. No trace of bitterness, this time.

'You know, when they built Stevenage after the war it was one of these New Towns,' she explained. 'Part of the government's plan to expand housing outside of London. It was very exciting. They had all these lovely big three-bedroom houses and well, we were all living in these cramped little London flats. They said to us: "Come to Stevenage and we'll give you a nice big council house. A big three-bedroom council house." Well, we came to visit and thought it was wonderful. So clean, so new! Big wide streets, lovely parks and the houses were huge compared to what we were used to in London. Your Grandad left the Navy and retrained in carpentry, so we moved here and I got my job in the Dairy. It wasn't long before Carol came along and then your mum and the boys. Well, it was a busy time but you know, Stevenage felt like such a good place. Good for kids, safe.'

Silence. Nan was so unhappy and I felt the same, deep inside me. I felt all the same things she did and here, with the two of us alone, I let myself cry the way I wanted to. Just large, sad tears dropping onto my sleeve, one after another. She held my hand and we cried together: for Mum, for Grandad and for ourselves. Things hadn't worked out the way Nan had wanted. Despite all those big dreams and big houses, she had lost the people she loved. And among the sadness and confusion of her grief, Nan also seemed angry and very, very disappointed that all those promises of a new life and a fresh start in Stevenage had come to this. She had travelled such a long way from her home in Newcastle in search of a better life and now all her hopes and dreams had turned to dust.

'Diane's here!' Dad announced brightly as he strode into the living room, where I was curled up with Tammy in my favourite spot on the sofa, watching *Blankety Blank*. It was Saturday night, a really good TV night, but Dad was off out to the cinema with his new friend, Diane, and now he stood squarely in front of the TV, blocking my view, so I sat up reluctantly to greet her. She strolled in casually, hands behind her back, her white leather handbag swinging by her ankles. Diane seemed young and punky to me – she wore her dark burgundy hair in short spikes, her stonewashed jeans were tight on her slim legs and the sleeves of her shiny red bomber jacket were pulled up to her elbows, exposing her collection of thick, clanking bangles. Her heels were white, to match her handbag.

'Alright, Amanda?' she said.

'Yeah, fine, thanks,' I replied automatically.

Nan Eve pushed herself up from her armchair now and fussed around, offering Dad and Diane cups of tea and slices of Battenberg cake, but Dad pointed to his watch and said they had to hurry because the film was starting soon.

There was some chatter now about the film they were going to see, whether it would last long and what time they would be back.

'Here, have a sit down,' Nan insisted to Diane, indicating the spot next to me. There was an awkward silence, then Diane lowered herself to the sofa on my right side and we exchanged brief smiles. Then I turned my attention back to Terry Wogan, who was reading aloud from a card in his hand:

'Our local fish and chip shop is run by an ex-hairdresser. He is so forgetful, he doesn't put salt and vinegar on the chips, he puts *BLANK* on them instead.'

'Hair dye!' shouted Grandpa Frank gamely from his side of the sofa.

I grinned.

'So.... erm, Amanda, how's school?' Diane asked me.

Looking at her closely now, I could see she wore pink shimmery make-up on her eyelids and her mouth was high-lighted by a dark red lipstick. She smelled strongly of perfume and her hair was almost shiny in the places where it stuck up straight in the air.

'It's fine, thanks,' I murmured.

Another long silence. Dad hopped impatiently from one foot to another then eventually, he blurted out: 'Okay, well, that was nice, wasn't it? Shall we go?'

And with that Diane bolted off the sofa and everyone said loud 'goodbyes' so that I still couldn't hear the TV. It was a relief when I finally heard the door slam and I could enjoy the show in peace. I loved Saturday nights in with my grandparents, each of us taking turns to shout at the

TV or make silly comments, as Tammy purred contentedly on my lap.

'You alright there, Amanda?' Nan Eve asked me after a few minutes.

I nodded; I was fine. I had settled myself right into the sofa now and felt warm and cosy. I was perfectly okay.

And that's the way I thought it would stay – living with Nan Eve, Grandad Frank and Dad, going to Peartree Infants School and seeing my Chalkley family at the weekends. But midway through January, Dad and Nan Eve sat me down to tell me I would be moving into a new house with Dad and Diane.

'I don't want to go,' I said quietly to my shoes. 'Can't I just stay here with you, Nan, and Grandad?'

'I'm afraid not, love,' Nan shook her head sadly.

I loved my Nan so much – she was soft and loving and the closest person I had to a mother. I liked being with my dad, he was fun and he took me out to the park where we ran around together, but we weren't close the way I was close to Nan. And I barely knew Diane.

'Can't I please just stay with you?'

Dad looked upset but I couldn't help it. I didn't want to leave my Nan's house – I felt safe here. But there was no persuading Nan. They had all made their minds up.

'He's your dad,' Nan said to me that night when she tucked me into bed. 'You should be with him. Trust me, everything will be okay and you won't be far from us. You can see us any time you like, I promise.'

I didn't say anything for a while. It was January now, just a month after Grandad Bill had died, and it felt like nothing in my life was for keeps. I wanted to believe Nan Eve, though – I wanted to be with her as long as possible. And somewhere deep inside me, as always, there was that tugging feeling at my heart – that feeling of just wanting my mum back again.

'Can I really come and see you whenever I want?' I asked her.

'Really. Whenever you feel like it. Your grandad and I, we'll always be here for you. Now close your eyes, love, and try to get some sleep. Tomorrow, we can show you your new house and your new bedroom! Your dad says you can even pick your own wallpaper. Won't that be lovely?'

She said all this as she tucked my duvet down against the sides of the bed, then patted it down around me. Then, with great effort and a lot of groaning, she pushed herself up to a standing position from where she knelt in front of my bed and started to walk towards the door.

'Nan!' I called. 'Will you... will you leave the light on in the landing tonight?'

She opened the door and nodded at me.

'Yes, of course, love. Don't worry, I'll leave the light on.'

Then she was gone.

CHAPTER 8

HER VOICE

Dad and I moved out at the end of January, just a week after they told me we were going to live with Diane. Right up until the day itself, I begged my nan and grandad to let me stay with them. Everything was moving too quickly for me and I felt myself becoming more and more anxious at nights. But they said they didn't have any choice in the matter and that because he was my dad, I had to go and live with him and Diane.

'It's not up to us, Amanda, love,' Nan Eve insisted.

But I couldn't take no for an answer. I had spent the last six months just getting used to being with Nan and Grandad and now it was all changing again.

We moved round the corner to 51 Wigram Way, which was about three minutes' walk from my nan's house. It was a two-bedroom house on a long street, with rows of houses facing each other on both sides. There was a front garden and steps leading up to the front door. Inside was a small hallway and stairs that went upstairs on the left side. Walking through the hallway we came to a living room with a large window on the far wall that looked out onto a good-sized back garden. The living room led to the kitchen and beyond that was a utility room with a window overlooking the back garden.

'Come on,' Dad said and took me by the hand and led me up the stairs. 'Let me show you your bedroom.'

He showed me into a medium-sized square-shaped room at the back of the house. I tried my best to make it feel like home – I put my teddies on my bed and unpacked all my clothes into the drawers, but still the place didn't smell warm and comforting the way my nan's house did. There was something cold about this new house and all of a sudden I felt very lonely.

The following Monday, Dad left early for work as usual, but instead of Nan Eve coming into my room to get me up for school, I heard an unfamiliar voice shouting: 'AMANDA!'

Diane was stood at the foot of the stairs, yelling: 'GET UP, AMANDA! TIME FOR SCHOOL!'

When I came downstairs, all washed and dressed in my uniform, she had the cereals out on the table. After I'd wolfed down a bowl of Rice Krispies, she hurried me into my navy duffel coat and we left the house together. Diane walked me to school that first day with my long caramel-brown hair swinging freely at my shoulders. I'd been too embarrassed to ask her to put my hair up. Usually, Nan Eve brushed my hair every morning and combed it into nice high bunches on either side of my head.

Diane only seemed to realise I needed my hair up once we got to the school gates and she saw all the other girls.

'Oh, Amanda! Have you got any hairbands on you?'

I shook my head.

'Oh well, I'm sure you'll be fine. It's only for one day. Go on then – off you go!'

She didn't come into the playground with me, like Nan Eve did – she just stood at the gates and left me to go in on my own.

Later that week, after school, Diane took me to the hairdresser's and got them to cut all my hair off so it was short and spikey, like a boy's. Like hers.

'That's better!' she grinned, as the hairdresser whipped the gown away with a flourish and swivelled my chair round to face her. 'Now you'll look really snazzy for school!'

I felt sick; I hated my new hairstyle. I missed Nan Eve brushing my hair and my jolly swinging bunches. I hated this new, punky style on me – it looked stupid.

From the very beginning, I had trouble sleeping at my new home. Most nights Dad took me up to bed, tucked me in with a kiss on the cheek and then whispered, 'Good night', before heading back downstairs. For a while, I'd lie in bed, waiting for sleep to claim me, but it never happened. Instead, I'd feel an overwhelming urge to get up and leave the room. I'd head to the landing, where I found myself drawn to the window. For some reason, looking out onto the street always made me feel better. The orange glow of the street lights, the warm light from the windows of other houses. Occasionally a car went past, but not often. Gradually I'd start to feel sleepy and then I'd try to go back to bed. But no sooner was I lying down than I'd feel the familiar cold dread in the pit of my stomach. *Go to sleep! Go to sleep!* I urged myself, my eyes screwed tight as if to block out these unwelcome feelings. I knew I should feel relaxed and tired, but I didn't; I was on edge, as if I had to do something urgently. So I'd jump up and rush to the window again.

Occasionally, Dad caught me.

If he had to go to the toilet, which was upstairs, he'd come out from the living room and say, in a surprised voice: 'What are you doing?'

'I couldn't sleep,' I'd say before returning to my room. Sometimes I stayed there, other times I went back to the landing. Eventually I'd drift off, only to wake up in the night to hear the man's voice in my head getting louder and louder. It would fade for a while before returning, loud again. His voice terrified me. I was so scared, I didn't know what to do. Everything seemed faster; my heart pumped faster, my face felt red and hot.

What to do? What to do? I have to do something. Quickly!

Petrified, I did the only thing I could think of: I got out of the room.

'Oh, not this again!' I heard Diane shout one night after I'd woken up in a panic and fled into the hallway, where I switched on the light.

Dad swung open their bedroom door in his paisley pajamas, his black hair sticking up everywhere, eyes squinting into the light.

'What's going on, Amanda?' he demanded.

'I got scared, Dad,' I gasped. I was still in the grip of the terror and I felt my chest rise and fall as I breathed hard. At least out here, I couldn't hear the man's scary voice.

'We've told you before, don't switch on the light!' he said tetchily.

'You woke us up!' Diane shouted from their bedroom. 'You woke us up again!'

'But I'm scared, Dad,' I said to him quietly. Usually when this happened at my Nan Eve's house, she would ask me what was scaring me and I'd tell her about the noise. Often she would take me to the window to see what the problem was, or she would go into my room herself to take a good look around. And listen for a man's voice. When she heard or saw nothing, she'd tell me that it was all fine, in a reassuring way, and put me back to bed. 'I've checked for myself and there's nothing there, dear,' she'd say, as I was led back to my bed.

But there was none of that with Dad.

'Oh, don't be silly. Everything's fine,' he muttered, then he turned around, switched off the light and headed back to his bedroom. 'Just go back to sleep.'

The following night, I had the same terrifying vision of the man coming out of the wall at me and I ran for the hallway. Without even thinking, I reached for the light switch. But when I flicked it up, nothing happened. Confused, and still terrified, I tried again. I flipped it up and down several times. *Why wasn't it working? What was wrong?* Thankfully, there was still a faint dusting of orange light from the streetlights outside, so I ran to the window and looked at the street below and the stars above, waiting for the calm to take over me and the panic to subside. Gradually, as my eyes grew used to the soft half-light, I walked to the middle of the hall corridor and looked up, under the lampshade of the overhead light: the bulb was gone.

They had taken out the bulb.

Still, life carried on. I got used to my new short hair and Diane's way of waking me up each morning. I loved going to school, so once I was there, I could just run around and play with the other children, forgetting all my worries about the nighttime and my new life. At school, I could be myself. Most of the kids there knew about what had happened to me, so when I started coming to school with Diane, they knew she wasn't my mother. If someone asked though, I was careful to set them straight.

'She's not my real mum,' I'd say solemnly. 'My real mum died in a fire.'

This was true: she *had* died in a fire. But I didn't add that she had died in a fire after being strangled to death – I didn't want to go into detail. It was so hard for me to talk about what happened with anybody, let alone people I didn't really know very well.

Thankfully, my scars were healing well and I was walking normally and wearing ordinary socks and shoes. The only evidence I'd been in the fire were the dark patches from the grafts and the white scars on my legs, but I tried not to let them hold me back. During PE I wore little shorts, just like all the other children, and I didn't feel shy about the way they

78

looked – I just loved running about and doing games. Nobody really looked at my legs anyway. The children in my school were kind and understanding. There was just one little boy who teased me.

'You've got burnt eggs!' he'd shout and point at my legs. He was in the year above me and I think he thought he was being really funny and clever by saying 'burnt eggs' instead of 'burnt legs'. I didn't think he was being either and when the rest of the children turned away from him in disgust, he stopped saying it.

School, for the most part, was my sanctuary.

Diane picked me up every afternoon and we went back home, where I would sit and watch TV while I did my homework until Dad got back at 5.15pm. There was little talk between Diane and myself when we were alone – she wasn't nasty, she just didn't have much to say to me. At teatime, Dad would talk to me about my day and if there was anything I needed to know, I asked him. At the weekends I would usually see either my Chalkley family or my Nan Eve and Grandad Frank. Sometimes Dad took me to the park and we liked to run about together, or we went swimming, just like we did before the move.

I didn't know anything about the baby until one day, three months after we moved in, I noticed Diane was looking very round in the middle.

'Why are you so fat now?' I asked simply. To me it seemed strange that she had only got fat in the middle of her tummy. Dad and Diane both laughed indulgently.

'That's not fat, silly,' he said to me. 'That's a baby in there. You're going to have a baby brother or baby sister.'

'Oh, I hope it's a baby sister!' I jumped in eagerly. I would have loved to have a baby sister to dress up and play with.

'Well, we'll just have to see, won't we?' said Diane, twirling her spaghetti bolognaise delicately around her fork. 'We don't know what we're expecting. We'll be pleased as long as the baby is healthy. Isn't that right, Dave?'

And my dad nodded his head. I'd noticed lately that he usually agreed with everything Diane said.

In March, a year after the fire, my Chalkley family took me to the grave where my mum was buried in Almond Lane Cemetery. It had been a whole year and it felt like forever! So much had changed in my life, I hardly felt like the same girl I was before. Though I tried desperately to hang onto my memories of Mum, already I struggled to remember the sound of her voice. It made me feel sad. Walking through the gravestones, though, I was cheered to see her headstone had a lovely photo of her in a pretty white frame, surrounded by pink and purple flowers.

My Nan Floss told me she came here a lot, especially after she lost my grandad – she did her best to keep it nice. Grandad was buried in the same cemetery, only a little further up, so after we had visited my mum, we visited Grandad too. Today, all the Chalkleys were here – my Uncle Mick, Aunty Carol, cousins Claire and Greg and Nan Floss, Uncle Kevin, Uncle Keith and his girlfriend Jane. Nan led the way, a bunch of fresh yellow carnations in her hand to fill the vase at the front of the grave.

'Oh, Sue, we've come to see you,' Nan murmured as we approached the gravestone. It was funny the way she spoke, just like a mum talking to her daughter. It made me feel like Mum was right there, listening to us, not dead at all.

'I've got some new flowers for you. Look, just the colour you like!' Nan picked up the vase, threw away the old stems and replaced them with the new ones. Then she put it down carefully on the gravestone and hitched up her skirt before kneeling down next to the headstone. She placed her hand gently on the stone, and started speaking.

'I know you're well, where you are, Sue,' she said sweetly. 'I'm sure you're up there, horse riding now with all your friends. Yes, I can see you having a lovely time up there...' On and on she would go, talking to my mother as if she was just sat across from her in the graveyard, listening. I never spoke out loud when I was at the gravestone with my family, though. I couldn't do that, not the way Nan Floss did, as if she was talking to someone right there. No, I spoke to her in my head:

I miss you, Mummy, I wish you were here. I hope I see you again one day.

A month later, I turned six. Dad took me out to the Lakes for the day and later on I went to stay with Nan Eve and Grandad Frank, which was lovely. The next morning, we had eggs for breakfast, just like old times, and then at 10am, Mick picked me up so I could spend some time with my Chalkley family. By the time I got home, I was laden with cards from all my different aunts, uncle and cousins. Dad's card, a picture of Minnie Mouse with a badge that said 'I am six!', was sat on the mantelpiece, right next to the card from Nan Eve and Grandad Frank, which had a cartoon picture of a teddy holding a balloon. I started lining up all my other cards next to theirs.

'What are you doing?' Dad asked when he came through from the kitchen. I was so pleased with my lovely row of cards that I just trilled: 'Ta da!' and gestured at the full mantelpiece. I felt very special, having so many cards. It was nice to think that so many people cared about me. But Dad didn't seem happy – he scowled at me, and at the row of cards behind me.

'I don't want those... *things* from your other family up in this house,' he snarled, pointing at all the cards from my Chalkley family. 'Take them down!'

'But... but... it's my birthday!'

'You heard what I said – take them down. NOW!'

'Well, what am I supposed to do with them?' I asked sulkily.

It didn't seem fair. Why did everyone have to be so angry at each other all the time? I hadn't done anything wrong. And yet here I was, stuck in the middle of it all.

'I don't care what you do with them! You can put them up in your bedroom, if you like, but I don't want to look at them in my living room. Okay?'

'Okay!'

I swept up the cards in my arms and stomped upstairs, cross with my dad. In my room, I lined the cards up again, this time on the little bedside table next to my bed. But here, alone, they didn't bring me quite so much joy.

I sighed.

Why did everything have to be so difficult? Why does it

have to be like this? For a second I thought about the fire – maybe it would have been easier if I'd died in the fire with Mummy. Then I'd be with her now, up in Heaven, just like Nan Floss said, happy and riding horses together...

NO!

Some little voice spoke inside my head now. It was a soft voice, a comforting, familiar voice. It sounded like... like my mother's voice! My eyes pricked with tears now as I recalled her soft tones exactly as I used to hear them.

It's going to get better, I heard her say. *One day, it's all going to get better. This is not forever. Be strong, Amanda, be strong, my little girl. I'm still here for you.*

I heard my mother saying my name and I collapsed into tears. Now I could sense her all around me – I felt her gentle touch, saw her heartbreaking smile and smelt her light, fresh scent. I could feel her; I could touch her. Now my mind, like a broken record player, returned to the memory of her that I held dearest: the memory that brought me the most happiness.

The memory of us... before.

CHAPTER 9

MAGIC

'Are you ready?' I called, breathless with excitement.
'Ready!' Mummy yelled back.

I ran into the living room and looked down into Mummy's hands. She was grinning at me as she lifted up the lid of the Milk Tray box.

All the chocolates in the plastic tray had disappeared! The box was completely empty.

'Ah!' I breathed in awe, peering down into the box. 'Where have they gone, Mummy? Did you eat them all?'

I put my hands to her face to prise apart her mouth. She let me tug at her jaws and fish around in her mouth for evidence of chocolates but no, there were none there. I looked all around her, pushing her bottom up from the sofa to see what she might have hidden underneath her, but nothing.

'Stop it!' she was laughing now as I crawled along on the

floor, lifting up her feet to check that she hadn't put them under there. 'There's nothing there, Amanda! Stop it – you're tickling me! I haven't hidden them, I promise!'

I was confused and got up again: 'But where have all the chocolates gone, Mummy?'

Mummy spread her hands apart and raised her eyebrows.

'Magic!' she breathed, her eyes wide open. 'It's magic! Now, go out to the hallway and I'll make them come back.'

So I ran out to the hallway and a second later, Mummy called me back in.

All the chocolates were back in the box!

I was awestruck.

'Wow, that's amazing! Mummy, how did you do it? How did you do it?'

I bounced up and down in front of her, begging her to tell me her secret trick.

'It's just magic!' she smiled, eyes twinkling. 'One day, I'll tell you. Now, go on, you can take the orange one, if you like. I know that's your favourite.'

I smiled to myself now, recalling the way my mum's beautiful face lit up when she was happy. Now that I was six years old, I knew how she had done it. I'd worked it out one day at my Nan Floss's house when I'd examined a half-eaten box of Milk Tray she'd left lying on the side table. You see, Milk Tray boxes usually have two layers of chocolates – one plastic tray on top and one underneath. Mummy's box of Milk Tray had an empty layer underneath and so she had just swapped the layers while I was out of the room. But to my four-year-old self, this was an incredible display of magical power.

I lay on my bed now and replayed this scene over and over again in my head. I looked at my mother from all angles, examining the shine on her long blonde hair, the twitch at the corners of her full lips as she tried to hide her delight, her pearly-smooth skin and the way she moved, slowly but with gentle purpose. I watched her laughing, throwing her head back to expose her long white neck, and then the way she looked at me, eyes sparkling, challenging me to work out the puzzle. And in that one little moment, I saw all the love she had for me, pouring out of her. And I had it now, here in my heart, captured forever like a genie in a bottle. Just like real magic, there was a sparkle of love hidden in that scene we shared, hidden from view, but still visible to me. A part of me was forever that little girl, entranced by her mummy's magical hands.

Don't forget, I told myself, *don't ever forget this.*

Now, here, hiding under my covers, I wished my mum had been properly magic – I wished she had been able to make herself disappear and reappear again. I was afraid that she would disappear forever from my mind and never come back again. I didn't want to lose her, so I clung to this memory and played it over and over again in my head, just for the rare chance to watch her smile and to bask in the warmth of her love.

'Are you ready?'

CHAPTER 10

WEETABIX

'Oh, he's beautiful!' I whispered into the see-through cot next to the hospital bed, putting out a hand to stroke my baby brother's tiny cheek. It was so soft and silky-smooth, like stroking water.

'Can I hold him, please?' I asked and my dad looked over to Diane, who lay in the hospital bed in her candy-striped dressing gown. She looked tired but very happy. She nodded at Dad.

'Okay, Amanda, why don't you go and sit on that chair and I'll bring him over to you?' said Dad, and so I scampered over to the blue leather chair in the corner of the hospital room.

It was June 1981 when my little baby brother Terry was born at the QE2 Hospital in Welwyn Garden City, not the Lister Hospital in Stevenage where I'd spent so much time recovering from the burns. Diane was quite particular about this – she had wanted my brother to be born in Welwyn because that was where her family lived. Dad drove me there to see him a few days after the birth. By the time I was in the room, faced with the tiny little boy with soft dark brown curly hair, I was beside myself with excitement.

Now, I sat solemnly on the chair, hands cradling my elbows, all ready to receive the baby. Dad leant over the cot and carefully lifted out my sleeping baby brother, then walked very slowly over to me, where he placed the little bundle in my arms.

He was surprisingly light, just like a tiny doll.

'Now, careful, Amanda,' Dad smiled, kneeling down to face me. 'You have to support his head like this,' and he moved my arms slightly so it was now under Terry's neck. 'Because babies can't hold their heads up themselves.'

I beamed with glee into the face of my baby brother. He was adorable, sleeping soundly in my arms, his little eyes scrunched up tight, a tiny fist balled at his face and rosebud lips pursed together. Each delicate finger on his hand seemed so small and yet perfectly formed. I examined his tiny fingernails, the deep creases at his knuckles and the pink, squidgy skin on the back of his hands with wonder. He was so new! I wondered if I had looked like this once. Suddenly, something occurred to me.

'Can he sleep in my room?' I asked them both and they burst out laughing.

'Not unless you're planning to get up in the middle of the night to feed him, Amanda!' Diane drawled, her voice slow and tired.

'Not yet, love,' said Dad, gently stroking my brother's hand. 'But after he gets a little bigger, yes, he can sleep in your room.'

YES! I had to stop myself from shouting it out loud. With my baby brother at my side, I knew there was no chance that the horrible man's voice would haunt me at night.

Once Diane and Terry were back home, things didn't quite settle down to normal, though. For one thing, Diane seemed to spend an awful lot of time sitting down with Terry, feeding him the bottle, her mind and thoughts always somewhere else. It was as if she went on a little journey in her head during these sessions and our day-to-day routine was a million miles from her thoughts.

'Diane, can I have my breakfast now, please?' I asked her one Monday morning after I had washed and dressed myself, ready for school. Since Dad left for work before we got up, it was up to Diane to give me my breakfast, a bowl of Rice Krispies or Weetabix.

'In a minute…' she replied absent-mindedly, sitting in the living room with Terry across her lap, his eyes closed as he sucked greedily from his bottle. I waited patiently and when it was nearly time to leave, I asked her again. I was all ready and waiting, sat at the kitchen table, as if to show her what I needed. My stomach growled with hunger.

'I said "in a minute"!' she replied tetchily this time.

But there were no more minutes left! I looked anxiously at the clock – *tick, tick, tick!* If I didn't leave soon, I'd be late for school. Silently, I watched the last few seconds tick by and still

Diane didn't move. My Weetabix box sat, undisturbed, in the cupboard, while I sat at the table, increasingly upset.

Finally, I burst out: 'It's time to go!' and jumped up to put on my duffel coat and collect my satchel. That morning I walked to school on an empty stomach, frustrated and upset that I hadn't had anything to eat. The whole morning I felt my stomach twist and yawn with hunger, but there was nothing to be done about it till milk-time, which filled me up till lunch.

The next morning, it was the same again... and the same after that.

This can't go on, I thought, *I have to do something or I'll never eat breakfast again!* So on Thursday, I left the house slightly earlier than usual and instead of walking straight to school, I hurried to my Nan Eve and Grandad Frank's house, which took only a few minutes. It was just 8am but knowing their routine so well, I was confident they would be up at this time. And, as she always said, Nan would be there for me, no matter what.

'Amanda!' Nan couldn't hide her surprise when she opened the door that morning.

'Morning, Nan!' I answered brightly.

'Isn't it time for school, love?' She seemed confused.

'Nearly...' I hesitated, looking down at my black Clarks shoes for a minute. 'Erm, I didn't have breakfast today. Could I have something here, please?'

'Oh!' Nan's face fell. 'Oh, of course you can. Come in, come in. I'll pop some toast in the toaster. Fancy an egg?'

Over warm, buttered toast and a runny soft-boiled egg,

I told Nan and Grandad what was happening with Diane at home.

'I think she's just got very forgetful, Nan,' I frowned, munching on a toasted soldier dripping with oozing yellow yolk. 'Because I do ask her and she does say she will get me my Weetabix, but then she just keeps forgetting. It must be the baby. I think the baby makes her forget.'

'Yes, well...' Nan chewed her lip and furrowed her brow as if she really didn't agree with me at all.

'Well, we don't want to upset her, do we?' she went on.

I shook my head. Grandad shook his head too.

'So why don't you just come here for your breakfast, then?' Nan smiled. 'If Diane's a little too busy with the baby, we'll make sure you get fed in the mornings.'

I shrugged. It seemed fine to me, though it did occur to me later, as I walked to school on a full belly for the first time that week, they could just *talk* to Diane for me! *Why don't they just ask her to give me breakfast again?* I wondered. In my head it was pretty simple – adults made things really complicated.

Nevertheless, we settled down into our new routine and for a while, I was very happy trotting off to my grandparents every morning for a satisfying breakfast of eggs, toast or a kipper.

'This is just our little secret,' Nan reminded me the second time I went there. 'Remember that, Amanda. We don't have to say anything to Diane about it.'

That was fine with me, though I still didn't quite understand why it was such a big deal. There was even a little plan in place, in case she turned up unexpectedly at the house: I was to run out the side door so that she didn't see me. It didn't seem likely – after all, she usually spent all morning sitting with Terry, staring into space, so I didn't think she would be up and about by the time I left for school.

And yet, three weeks after our new arrangement, it happened.

Just as I was polishing off a lovely scrambled egg one morning, we heard the click of the front door lock and Diane's voice as she let herself in.

'It's only me!' she called out. I had been at the table, wolfing down the last of my egg, when suddenly, I jumped up out of my chair.

OH, MY GOD, DIANE!

Nan's eyes widened in shock.

'Quick!' she hissed. 'Grab your coat. Run out the back! *RUN!*'

So I legged it, as fast as I could through to the kitchen and from there out the back door, my duffel coat in my hands, mouth still full of egg. Once outside, I sprinted down the road as fast as I could and didn't stop until I had made it safely round the corner. Then I stopped and for a moment I stood still, shaky and tearful, just waiting to catch my breath while I put my coat on. *Had she seen me? Did Nan manage to cover for me?* She must have realised someone was there because of my plate and the way I'd left the house, banging the side door on my way out.

Oh, God, what was going to happen now?

All day long, I was tormented by the thought of what Diane would do to me when I got home. I didn't know why it had

94

to be a secret like this and was confused and upset about the whole situation. I mean, it was only breakfast! It wasn't as if I'd done anything bad or naughty.

'Yes, she saw you,' Nan confirmed when I popped in to see her on the way home that afternoon.

My heart froze in my chest. *What would happen to me now?*

Nan tried her best to be reassuring.

'It's alright,' she said. 'I told her you were just hungry and that's why you were round here. I don't think she realised there was a problem…'

But I shook all the way home and finally, when I knocked on the door that afternoon, I felt my stomach flip with nerves. My heart was heavy and full of dread.

The door swung open – Diane towered over me, her face hard with anger.

For a brief second there was silence. Then her hand came down and I felt a sharp, hot sting on top of my left ear.

'What do you think you're playing at?' she demanded. 'Get inside! Go on, inside. *Now!*'

I scampered indoors, hoping that was the worst of it. But once in the living room she stood, hands on hips, head tilted to one side, her face contorted with fury.

'What do you think you've been up to?' she snarled. 'Going there in the morning? You're meant to go straight to school!'

'There was no breakfast,' I stammered, holding my throbbing ear. 'I was going there for breakfast.'

'I could see you were having your breakfast there!' she barked at me. 'I could see that very well indeed! But you are supposed to eat breakfast here in the mornings. I might have to feed your baby brother but you should just jolly well wait! Have you heard of patience? I've got a lot on my plate here! Babies need to eat too!'

'I couldn't wait,' I objected. 'I was going to be late for school.'

Despite being scared of Diane, I stood my ground.

'That's not true,' she retorted. 'You've been racing out of here early every bloody morning, well before the school bell.'

'I only started doing that after you forgot to give me my breakfast the first few times. Not in the beginning.'

'Right, well, you can stop that right now. You're not to disturb your nan in the morning again. Got it?'

I nodded, then she waved her hand as if dismissing me and I raced upstairs to my room, desperate to get away from her. *Thank God that was over!* It was horrible and I hated getting told off by Diane. When I went down to breakfast the next morning, the box of Weetabix was already on the table. I was pleased. It was a relief that I didn't have to sneak around anymore and at least now I would be fed in the mornings.

'Now that we're a family, you should call Diane "Mum",' said Dad.

I froze. Beside me my six-month-old brother carried on giggling and blowing raspberries at me, just as I had been doing to him a few seconds before, unaware of my sudden change in mood. Dad wanted me to call Diane 'Mum'? I felt wretched.

'But she's not my mum,' I whispered under my breath.

Diane sat at the other end of the table, nodding approvingly at Dad.

'Is that clear?' Diane asked. She hadn't heard me, thank God.

'Yeah, fine,' I murmured into my plate and carried on eating.

She told him to say this, I thought. *It didn't come from him.* But it didn't feel right and I hated having to call her 'Mum'. I only did it when nobody else could hear me – I didn't want other children to think she was my real mum. If they thought she was my birth mum, they would never know the truth. I knew why she wanted me to do it – so we would look more like a normal family to other people. But she didn't *feel* like a mum to me. She never hugged or kissed me, or gave me any reason to share my thoughts or feelings with her. It was as if she was happy keeping me at a distance, and that was fine by me too. We were like sisters in the same house, nothing like mother and daughter.

Strangely, despite her wish for us to be seen as a family, she didn't seem to include me in their visits to her parents in Welwyn. When Terry was a very small baby, we would go there all together, but after a while, Diane suggested they make the trip to her parents on the weekends when I was at my Chalkley family.

She didn't realise how hurtful it was when she said to my dad one day: 'We'll go when Amanda's on a visit because then it can be a special thing for us to do with Terry.' I felt left out of their little family unit, the three of them doing 'special things' together without me. I was never jealous of Terry – he was my baby brother and I loved him with all my heart – but his arrival marked a change in the way Diane treated me. Now, I didn't see her parents at all anymore and Dad never argued or questioned this. As usual, he just went along with whatever she said.

As the months passed, I preferred to spend my time outside of the house, playing with my friends on the big green on the corner of our street or in Pear Tree Park. But Diane didn't always like me to play outside. I found this confusing: some days, she let me go out and other days she decided I wasn't allowed to play out and that was the end of it.

'No, you're not going out today,' she'd puff haughtily.

'Why not?'

'Because I said so, that's why. Now, stop arguing and just do as you're told!'

It seemed crazy to me. Did she really think I was better off inside watching TV than outside playing in the fresh air? I loved going out on my roller skates or making up imaginary games about goodies and baddies with my pals. It wasn't as if there seemed to be any real reason for her objection. The green outside our home where I played with my friends was safe, well maintained and visible from most of the houses. Pear Tree Park wasn't far and there we had swings, a climbing frame, a roundabout and two slides – one big and one small. The tall one was really high and we all loved climbing up right to the narrow seat at the top, from where we'd go flying all the way down again. My friends and I were careful not to play in the road and we always came in for tea at the right time – none of us were naughty children. It felt like I was being punished but I didn't know why.

'It's not fair,' I'd grumble to her later, when I saw my friends playing. Was it simply that she didn't want me to have too much fun? Did she enjoy making me suffer like this?

'Well, that's the decision I've made so that's that,' she'd reply tartly, and that was indeed that.

Dad had a friend at work whose daughter was a few years older than me. The family were quite well-off and always bought lovely clothes from shops like Benetton, Gap and Tammy Girl. Every few months they had a clear-out and Dad would come home from work, arms laden with gorgeous clothes he'd picked up cheaply from his mate – corduroy trousers, leggings, denim jackets and little ra-ra skirts, T-shirts with Minnie Mouse on the front and animal print jumpers. They were all the latest fashions and I loved having new clothes to wear at the weekends. But one day, Diane put a stop to it.

'You've got to stop buying her all those unnecessary extra clothes,' she told him at teatime. She jabbed her fork in my direction. At this my cheeks burnt with embarrassment and anger. I hated the way she talked about me like that, right in front of my face, as if I wasn't there.

'She's got plenty of things to wear – she doesn't need to clog up her wardrobe with a load of extra tat. Besides, we can't afford it. If you're going to buy clothes for anyone, buy them for the baby.'

Dad just grunted in reply, but I knew he would do what she said and from now on, there would be no more extra clothes for me. He never went against Diane once she had made her mind up and I knew why: she had a very hot temper. She would fly off the handle for the tiniest little thing and it was quite scary at times.

The following year, I was selected for the netball team and invited to go to after-school netball practice. I was desperate to go, but when I asked Diane she said no.

'Why not?'

'Because Terry can't do it,' she said simply and returned to folding the washing.

What? *WHAT?* This didn't make any sense at all. Of course he couldn't do netball practice!

'But Terry's a baby!' I said dumbly. *Why was she bringing Terry into this?* Of course, he couldn't do netball – he could barely get from one side of the room to another without tripping over his own feet!

'It doesn't matter, you're not doing it and that's the end of it.'

'But...' I was boiling over with outrage and frustration.

'THAT'S ENOUGH! I've said "no" so don't argue. And don't give me that look! Unless you're going to take that miserable look off your face, you can go straight to your room, madam!'

It was at times like this I got so angry and upset, all I could do was run upstairs to my bedroom and cry into my pillow. There was no arguing with Diane once she had made up her mind and nobody in my family – not my nan or grandad and certainly not my dad – was prepared to challenge her. I just didn't understand; why did she make life so difficult for me? At times, it felt as if she really didn't like me – but why? I hadn't done anything to her, I was just a child – it was only netball practice, for goodness' sake! What on earth was wrong with me doing that?

Was it really worth it? I wondered in my darkest moments. *Was it really worth surviving the fire for this?* All the fighting between my two families, all the confusing and upsetting rows with Diane... Maybe if I died too, if I just threw myself through the window, I could be with my mum again. For a brief second, the thought comforted me, but then I knew I could never go through with it. For one thing, I knew my death would destroy my Nan Floss. She often said that she wouldn't have survived, had I been killed too. Me being alive now made things so much more bearable for her. I still loved spending time with Floss. And as time went on, it got easier to talk to her about Mum without feeling sad and she often told me nice things about her. In her house, my mother Susan came alive for me.

One day, when I was nine, I went round there and we were talking about Mum's love of animals. She had had a dog she adored called Dandy and was so horse-mad she drew a big picture of a horse on her walls. Later, when she was thirteen, Floss and Bill bought her a real white horse called Sherry. Mum was crazy about Sherry, who was stabled in a little village not far from her home.

'She rode her everywhere,' Floss smiled, shaking her head at the memory. 'You know, she even used to ride him down to the shops. God, the looks she used to get! But she didn't care, Susan. She just adored being on that horse. And she was a good rider too – won herself some rosettes.'

For a moment, Nan was lost in the memory, watching her daughter trotting off to the newsagent's on the back of her white horse. Then something occurred to her and she looked down at me, her hand on my arm.

'Here, I found something the other day. I reckon you should have it. Wait here.'

And with that, Floss disappeared out the room. I heard the floorboards creaking upstairs as she moved from room to room. Then she reappeared with a triumphant look on her face, clutching a 45 record. The cover had a very odd-looking, thin-faced man on the front, wearing eyeliner, red blusher and a shiny orange top. I had never seen a man who looked so strange and sad at the same time.

'It used to be your mum's,' she said. 'She loved it. Drove us both mad playing it over and over again! It was just sitting there, in her old cupboard, and I saw it and thought to myself: "Well now, I think Amanda should have that." So here it is.'

She handed me the record and I read the words on the front in stark yellow capital letters:

LIFE ON MARS
DAVID BOWIE.

Next to that, my mum had written her name in swirly letters: Susan Lowson.

I couldn't wait to get it home to play it.

CHAPTER 11

A MESSAGE
FROM MARS

The sad opening lines of 'Life On Mars' pierced through the silence of my bedroom like a streak of lightening in a black night sky. I sat there, mesmerised, as the room filled with David Bowie's stringy, otherworldly voice, backed by a simple piano accompaniment. I could picture the little girl in the song perfectly, the girl who walked through a sunken dream, who was hooked on the silver screen.

Suddenly the song started to build. A low note growled from a cello as Bowie's voice lifted – now, it was loud and angry, high and strong, like a hurt animal wailing in pain, wailing at the terrible things in the world.

I couldn't understand it all – the words were unusual, like nothing I'd ever heard before – but I loved it. It was like listening to a person who didn't understand life either, who couldn't make sense of it all, and I knew this was how I felt.

And once, this was how my mum felt too. This was a song that made me want to cry and laugh at the same time. It made me realise the world was mad and didn't always make sense. As the final line of the chorus rose up, I wanted to join in, to sing out loud 'Is there life on Mars?'

I listened all the way through to the end and when it had finished, I picked up the arm of the record player and put it back to the beginning and played it all over again. This time I listened harder and the words came through to me more. Again, once it was over, I played it again, and again and again. I couldn't stop playing it, just as my mum had done all those years before me. Because sitting here, listening to this weird, angry song, this song filled with cavemen and lawmen, sailors and Mickey Mouse, I felt connected to my mother, Susan Lowson. She had loved this record, she had written her name on the sleeve. Just like me, she had sat here and heard these words, and felt that stirring when the driving chorus and drumbeats kicked in, tugging at all her emotions at once. I could feel her heart then, just like mine, soaring up through the bars of the song, and in that moment, it felt like our two hearts joined together, beyond time, space and existence. In that moment, in this very special way, I could be with my mum again.

I hung onto this feeling when things got hard.

As I got older, I heard and understood more about my mother. She had been young when she married, just twenty years old. Looking at the wedding album of my parents' wedding at Nan Floss's house, I could see the innocence in her fresh face. And behind the eyes, hesitance, fear even. In many of the photos she was hardly smiling at all; there was just the slight suggestion upwards at the corners of her mouth. She was happy to be marrying my dad, I knew she loved him – as Nan Floss told me many times – but there was also a sense of uncertainty in her eyes. Did she have a feeling? Did she know that this wasn't destined to be her happy ever after? I still didn't understand why – and I didn't feel able to talk to Dad about it – but for some reason, it hadn't worked out. They had split up, and she was left alone to look after me not long after my second birthday.

Sometimes Aunty Carol would get out photos of my mum and press me to look at them with her. I could tell what she was trying to do – she wanted me to talk about my mum, to talk about my memories of her. She thought it would help me, but I didn't like doing this.

'Look at your mum there,' she'd say pointing to a picture of her face. 'Looks sad, doesn't she? She was sometimes a bit sad with life, your mum.'

Aunty Carol had very definite ideas.

'She's happier now,' she went on firmly. 'She's up there, in Heaven, with Dad, and she's much happier.'

At first, I didn't really understand why this bothered me so much. But as I got older, I worked it out. It was as if Aunty Carol assumed my mum wasn't able to *feel* happiness when she was alive and that being dead was better for her because life couldn't make her happy. It annoyed me because it assumed that Mum, even if she was sad sometimes, couldn't ever be properly happy in life. And that wasn't true. I knew she loved her horses, she loved music and she loved me. If you love stuff that much, if you feel so much love in your heart, you can surely be happy in life!

But Carol had found her own way to accept Mum's death. I knew she was just as torn up as the rest of us, but her ideas gave my mum's death more sense, more logic. It made her feel better about losing her little sister. But I could not accept that.

So no, I didn't want to look at pictures with Carol and tell her my memories. I didn't want to share the precious moments I had with my mum because I didn't want Carol putting her own thoughts in the way of them. I didn't want her ideas or interpretations spoiling them for me: I knew what I knew.

'Don't you want to remember your mum?' Carol sometimes got frustrated with me. 'I could tell you funny stories about her when she was little, if you like?'

'No, that's alright,' I'd reply meekly.

I'd heard some of Carol's stories before. She was the older sister, so her view of Mum was that of watching a younger sister growing up. That was her point of view. Susan Lowson was my mother so I had a completely different view of things. I was quite happy not to hear Carol's stories. Trying to stop everyone telling me their thoughts, memories and perspectives all the time was a bit stifling. I just wanted to be left alone to cherish my own memories.

Other people, they could be so frustrating! Even my lovely, caring cousin Claire could be insensitive. As we got older, she started to compare herself in looks to my mother.

'It's funny how I resemble Susan more, and you look more like my mum,' she'd say, hardly stopping to think how that might hurt me. She was *my* mother, not Claire's! But, like so much else, I just let it go. I didn't make a big deal out of it. After all, Claire wasn't aware that her words might hurt me and I didn't want to make her feel bad about it when she didn't mean any harm.

Even when a girl at school said: 'I know why you've got burns on your legs, you ran through a fire', I didn't correct her. I didn't want to talk about it, so I simply shrugged and walked away. She didn't mean to upset me – she just didn't know any better – and I suppose I learned that I couldn't control what people thought. As with Carol, I had to accept that people had their own ideas, their own thoughts, and I wasn't in control of them.

At times like this, I'd go home and play my mother's song, 'Life On Mars', on the record player, staring out of the window. It was so special to me to have this way to connect to my mum while she was on earth. When I heard the music my mother came to me, so real and so strong that I'd feel a painful twinge in my heart that I couldn't just reach out and touch her again. But it didn't last. Later on, out playing with my friends, I'd forget about what had been said and I'd laugh and run like I didn't have a care in the world.

It was true. We all had our sad moments, we all felt life was a God-awful small affair at times. But it didn't mean we couldn't be happy the rest of the time.

I knew that for a fact.

CHAPTER 12

BARRY
ISLAND

My heart thudded with excitement as I clambered onto the coach. Nan Eve stretched up on tiptoes on the pavement, waving maniacally at me, and Dad stood next to her, grinning away. I made my way up the aisles, past all my chattering Junior 4 classmates. The atmosphere was electric. Everyone was shouting and laughing, exchanging last-minute waves with their parents, sharing the contents of their lunchboxes and making a real racket.

'Amanda!' My friend Jane waved to me from the back of the coach. Jane was a bit of a tomboy with her short hair, khaki green trousers and trainers. Today, she wore a bright orange hooded parka. 'Come on!'

I pushed past the last of the rows of seats and took my place between her and my friend Maggie, casually dressed in a blue and grey tracksuit. Maggie, who was black, always had her hair braided in sweet little cornrows, and had the loudest laugh in the whole class. Though we looked very different, it was always the three of us and we'd been looking forward to this day for weeks. I gave one last little wave to Nan and blew a kiss to Dad, then turned round to face my friends. At last – we were off!

It was my last year in primary school and the first I knew about the proposed trip was when Diane asked me in the living room three weeks before if I'd like to go. For a moment, I was lost for words. It was so rare to be asked if I wanted to do things. Usually it was the other way round!

'There's a trip with the school,' she read from a piece of paper that had come out of my school bag that afternoon. 'To Barry Island in Wales. For a week in the Easter Holidays. Is that something you'd like to do, Amanda?'

'Oh, yeah!' I answered enthusiastically. I relished the idea of going on holiday with all my friends. 'That sounds fun.'

'All right,' said Diane. Then she turned to my dad: 'Well, you can use Amanda's fund for that.'

'Okay then,' said Dad, barely looking up from the TV.

Suddenly, I was confused.

'What fund?' I asked.

'They had a whip-round at my work,' Dad explained. 'You know, after the fire. We've been keeping the money safe for you, for something like this for you to do. It'll pay for the holiday.'

'Oh, right,' I nodded. Yeah, that sounded fine except... except I'd never heard of this fund before. It seemed strange nobody had mentioned it. I guess I was pleased that it meant I could go away with my friends, but at the same time I wondered why I hadn't been told about it, why I hadn't been given any choice on how it was spent.

Still, nothing could dampen my spirits at going away with my best pals, and we laughed and sang all the way to Wales. Once there, we spilled out onto the large Butlins complex and were shown to our individual chalets. It felt so grown-up to be given our own little chalet to share – me, Jane and Maggie. There was a bathroom, a living room with a bed, and another side room with bunk beds in it. We quickly chose our sleeping arrangements – Jane had the bed on its own in the living room and me and Maggie shared the bunk beds. For the first half an hour we just careered around the chalet, opening cupboards and exploring the rooms. This was amazing; this was freedom!

That afternoon our class was set a competition on the beach. In our designated chalet teams, we all had to dig a hole in the sand. The team that dug the biggest hole in half an hour would win a prize.

'Come on!' Maggie yelled, as she threw herself on her knees and started digging with the yellow plastic spades we'd been given. Jane and I quickly joined her and soon there was sand flying everywhere.

'We want to win this prize!' Maggie puffed, as she threw sand behind her.

'Yeah, let's make it really, really big!' I agreed. After about twenty minutes we'd created a large crater in the sand, big enough for us all to sit in while we carried on digging.

'Come *on*!' Maggie urged, as I sat back on my heels. I was exhausted and I wanted to see how we were getting on compared to the other teams, but from where we were, inside our hole, I couldn't really see the others.

'Keep digging!' I said. 'I'm going to go and check the other holes.'

So I left Maggie and Jane burrowing away while I walked up the sandy beach to check out the other holes. I crept up to each hole from behind the diggers, being careful not to alert them to my presence, and one by one, peered into the other children's holes.

Brilliant, I thought, as I peeked into the final hole. *They're none of them as good as ours! We're definitely going to win this.*

I bounded back to my team, full of beans and ready to pass on the good news, but as I returned and I saw Maggie's anxious face, I decided to have a bit of fun.

'Well?' she asked impatiently, shielding her eyes from the sun as she looked up at me from the depths of our hole. 'What are they like?'

'Oh, Maggie,' my face fell, my voice full of doom. 'They're all really deep holes.'

'You *what*?' Maggie exploded. 'Right, that's it – we're going to have to dig for our lives!'

And with that she went mental, digging as if there was no tomorrow. Jane was also going for it, but nothing like Maggie, who seemed to be completely possessed! It was all I could do to stop myself cracking a smile but I managed to keep it together and look serious. Finally, after Maggie had completely knackered herself out on our hole, the teacher blew the whistle and we all got the chance to inspect everyone else's work.

As Maggie, Jane and I walked past all the others, we saw our hole was about ten times bigger than everyone else's. I couldn't hide it any longer – I started to smile.

'These holes are *tiny*!' Maggie exclaimed in surprise and that's when I fell about laughing.

'Oh, Maggie!' I laughed. 'I couldn't help it, you were so serious about the digging and we were already miles ahead of them all. You should have seen yourself, going mad out there in the hole.'

'You cow!' she said, mock outrage in her eyes.

'It's true, you went like the clappers,' said Jane. 'I couldn't keep up!'

For a moment Maggie stared at me, but already I was laughing so hard I could barely stand up. Then she buckled and started to laugh too. The three of us rolled around in the sand, laughing so hard we nearly missed the grand prize-giving: 'And the winners are... Maggie, Jane and Amanda! Come up and get a stick of rock each.'

That set us off all over again. All that effort – for a stick of rock!

Later that night, after dinner, we went to the disco in the main hall with all the other children – there were about six different schools, each with classes of about forty kids, and it was really exciting being with so many other kids our age. My friends and I loved dancing and we made up little routines, which some of the other kids tried to copy. Then we fell into bed, exhausted. Thankfully, I didn't have any problems with nightmares because Maggie said we could keep the light on all night.

The rest of the week was amazing. We got to do lots of activities like fencing, archery, basket weaving, painting and even abseiling. Abseiling was a bit scary.

Usually I was fearless, but once I got to the top of the climbing wall and was told I would have to walk off it backwards, I felt my tummy go all funny.

'What, just walk off backwards?' I said. 'Without being able to see anything?'

'It's fine, Amanda,' said the instructor as he strapped me into the harness and tightened the chin strap of my helmet. 'Just remember what we taught you in the lesson – how to feed the rope from your hip to your hand and jump at the same time. You'll soon get the hang of it.'

I made a silent 'eek!' face to Maggie and Jane, who just shook their heads with fear. It was at times like this that I regretted always volunteering to go first!

Slowly and carefully, I inched my way to the edge of the wall, feeling the tension in the rope and gradually letting it out to allow myself to go further back. This was terrifying! I prayed that the rope was really strong and wouldn't snap.

'Remember, Amanda, you are in control the whole time,' the instructor called out as I started to disappear off the edge, feeling the strong pull of gravity towards the ground. 'You can push off and let out the rope at the same time, giving you a nice gentle descent.'

So I did as I was told, pushing off from the wall with my

feet and letting out the rope at my waist at the same time. For a moment I felt myself flying backwards and then, almost like a swing, I rebounded back onto the wall. I landed softly on the wall and instinctively bent my knees on landing, like a frog. Oh, this was lovely! Feeling more confident, I repeated the movement and now I let out the rope a little more so I felt myself gently descending as I swung out and back. I did four more push-outs with my feet and then, unbelievably, I was down on the ground!

The instructor at the bottom grabbed the rope above me as I stood up.

'That was great, Amanda,' she said. 'You really got the hang of it there. How do you fancy another go?'

'Yes, please,' I gasped. What a thrill! It felt amazing to abseil and I couldn't wait to do it again.

I loved the craft activities as much as the physical, outdoorsy ones. Learning to weave baskets was a challenging, consuming and ultimately very satisfying task. Carefully, I threaded my reeds in and out of my base structure, carefully pushing them down onto the weave to create the close-knit and secure basket. I wanted to make a really beautiful gift for my Grandad Frank – he was an engineer so I knew he would appreciate it. Most nights, Jane, Maggie and me mucked about in our chalet, being silly, trying on each other's clothes, singing Madonna songs to each other, having Polo mint fights and generally enjoying the freedom of being without adult supervision. At the disco, we'd all be watching each other to see who was trying out any new dances. I ALWAYS danced to Madonna – she was my very favourite artist and when I found out that she had lost her mum too when she was young, I felt a strong bond with her. We had both experienced great loss very young, but look at Madonna now! She had done so well for herself and was so full of energy and positivity. In every sense, she was my idol.

'So… erm, do you want to dance with me?'

The offer came from Declan, one of the cool boys at the disco. Inside, I was jumping up and down with delight that he had asked me to dance instead of any of the other girls. After all, Declan was really very handsome with dark brown hair, flicked over to one side, and wore a cool white jacket like Don Johnson from the *Miami Vice* TV series and baggy blue jeans. He was so cool, it hurt!

'Yeah, alright,' I replied casually. I didn't want to seem too keen. So we slow-danced to Madonna's new song, 'Live To Tell'. He held my shoulders and I put my hands on his waist. Slowly, we rocked from side to side and I tried not to catch Jane and Maggie's eyes, or I knew I would burst out laughing. Afterwards, Declan and I smiled and each returned to our friends, who were standing on the side of the hall.

'Wow!' said Jane, when I got back. 'You looked really cool out there.'

'Yeah? I like him,' I said. 'He smells nice, like soap.'

I couldn't wait to get back to the disco the following night so I could dance with Declan again. *Oh, Declan*! I flopped around the chalet that day, daydreaming about him. He was so handsome, with his piercing blue eyes hiding behind that dark, flicky fringe. I loved his name too – it was so unusual, so exotic. I'd never met anyone called Declan before. But that afternoon Jane, Maggie and I got into trouble for not cleaning up our chalet. Twice that week we were instructed to tidy up for an inspection, but in all the excitement of the activities, the discos and the sheer fun of being left alone to look after ourselves, we'd completely forgotten. When Miss Watts, our teacher, came to inspect our chalet in the middle of the afternoon, the place was a jumble of dirty clothes, hairbrushes, scrunchies, shoes, sweet wrappers and empty Coke cans.

'This is a state, girls!' Miss Watts exclaimed. 'What happened here?'

'Oh, no!' I whispered, suddenly remembering the inspection.

'We forgot,' Maggie said, shaking her head. 'We didn't know it was today, Miss!'

'Then you weren't paying attention at breakfast!' Miss Watts scolded. 'I made it very clear you should clean your room up today. I'm sorry, girls, but this is unacceptable. No disco for you tonight!'

That night after dinner Jane and Maggie and I sat at our chalet window, watching all the other children skipping off to the disco, and our hearts broke.

'Oh, no!' I sobbed, real tears falling down my face. 'Look at them all going to the disco without us. I wonder if Declan will ask someone else to dance now?'

Jane clung to my shoulder, devastated, too upset to even talk.

'They're all leaving!' Maggie cried, tears streaming down her face.

'Don't forget us!' I called out dramatically.

'No – don't forget us!' the other two echoed, and within a few minutes the last of the children had disappeared into the hall.

Our sadness didn't last long, though. Within a few minutes we had completely forgotten about the disco and were making up dance routines to 'Papa Don't Preach', using hairbrushes as microphones, trying our hardest to copy the Queen of Pop's complicated dance moves. After a while we even started giggling at how stupid we had been for crying about not going to the disco.

'We're such a bunch of idiots!' I grinned, falling back onto one of the sofas in the living room.

'*You're* an idiot, you mean!' Maggie teased.

'*You're* an idiot!'

'Oh, Declan!' Jane mimicked, throwing her head back in a mock swoon.

'Declan! Declan!' Maggie joined in and the pair started play-smooching their hands.

'Mwah! Mwah!'

'Stop it!' I shouted, laughing. And then we were all rolling around the floor, laughing our heads off.

It was the best holiday of my life. I had never felt so free and relaxed. On the coach on the way home, I stared at the rain lashing at the window and a heavy melancholy settled on my heart. I was sad the holiday was over and also sad to be leaving our little world of children. It had been such a relief to be out of the house for a week, away from all the adults in my life, a world full of strain and tension. All week long, I had laughed my head off and at night, Maggie let me keep the light on. I didn't even have to explain why – she just said yes and that was that. Even getting into trouble wasn't bad when I was with my friends, since we were all equal, all in it together. For the first time in a very long while, I hadn't felt at all lonely, I didn't feel alienated from other people. And unlike some of my classmates who had, at various points in the holiday, crumpled into tears, I hadn't missed home one bit.

That summer I finished primary school and I was sad to say goodbye to many of my friends, children I'd grown up with since the age of five. But at least I knew some of them would be going to the same secondary school as me, Heathcote Senior. Thankfully, I got to see lots of my school friends in the summer holidays too as we all went to the play scheme at Pear Tree Park. There, they ran arts and crafts workshops in the mornings and there was a table tennis and pool table, where we played in the afternoon. Twice a week, the club ran hockey games and we all ran around with plastic yellow and red hockey sticks, whacking inexpertly at the puck.

One day I was at home when my Aunty Carolyn and Uncle Melvin came over for a visit. Melvin asked me how I was getting on at school and I explained that I had just left and was about to start my new secondary school.

'Oh, so it's all change for you, then!' he smiled. 'I guess I'll be seeing you at the wedding.'

'What wedding?' I didn't know what he was talking about.

Melvin smiled at me as if I was making a joke: 'What wedding? Your Dad and Diane's wedding, of course!'

'Oh, yeah!' I smiled, like I was in on the joke. 'Yeah, course I'm going to that.'

I just said yes, but I really didn't know what was going on. That was just what it was like at my house. I didn't get told much and usually, if I asked, I was brushed aside with an abrupt 'I don't know, just wait and see'. So over time, I learned not to ask. Nobody had talked to me about a wedding, so I just waited until it happened.

Dad and Diane had a small wedding at the registry office in Stevenage's Old Town Hall over the summer. Diane wore a bright red dress and they bought me a pale blue dress for the occasion – it matched Terry's little blue pageboy outfit. Nan Eve and Grandad Frank came, as did Melvin and Carolyn, Diane's parents, her sister Linda and brother David, but other than that there were only a couple of friends there. Afterwards, Terry and I went back to our Nan's house for the evening. Before we left, Dad asked me if I had enjoyed myself and I said yes, but it was a lie. The truth was, I had missed my mum. I didn't even know why – it just felt strange to be watching my dad and Diane getting married. I recalled the pictures of Mum in her ivory wedding gown, the black velvet choker at her neck; her long blonde hair swept up behind her head and held in place with white flowers. Then there was the sweet crocheted shawl she wore on her shoulders for the pictures taken outside on what looked like a cold, grey day. And the pink and white bouquet she held in her hands.

That was the wedding I wanted to go to.

Yes, it was 'all change' as Melvin said, and I didn't know if

I felt ready for what came next. At night, I worried about the future: I wondered if my friends at my new school would be nice and if anything would change now that Diane and Dad were married. As I closed my eyes and tried not to think of The Man's Voice, I worried about what would happen tomorrow...

CHAPTER 13

A PLACE
TO GO

'Oh, it's you,' Diane said dully, her face half hidden by the door, which she had only opened a little way. Now she let it swing open fully as she disappeared inside the house. I walked in behind her and shut the door. This was how she greeted me every day after school. Every day it was the same: 'Oh, it's you' and then bam, she was gone.

I was never allowed my own house key, which was odd because all my other friends had them. Every day I walked to school and back on my own, so it would have made sense for me to have a key, but Diane objected to this.

'She doesn't need a key,' she told my dad. 'Besides, I don't want her in the house on her own.'

Dad just shrugged, though I did try and raise it with him later. I didn't understand why she thought it wasn't a good idea for me to be able to let myself in. This was my home too – why couldn't I let myself in after school? What did she think I was going to do with a key? Lose it, sell it... give it to house burglars?

I appealed to him.

'It's not worth fighting about,' he insisted. 'Just drop it.' So now I had to ring the bell every single day I got home, only to be faced with Diane's grumpy response.

The first few times she answered the door I attempted a chirpy 'Hi!' but I gave this up very early on. It was exhausting, trying to be nice in the face of such overwhelming indifference. Sometimes I felt like replying: 'Yes, well, incredibly, I do go to school and then finish at the same time *every single day*, which means that even more incredibly, I arrive home at the same time *every single day*. So the chances of it being me at the door are rather great, aren't they? It's not likely to be anyone else!'

I trudged up the stairs as Diane disappeared into the kitchen, still mulling over her daily surprise at my arrival. I mean, who was she expecting to see roll up at the doorstep at this time of day, the Prime Minister of Britain? Did she think Margaret Thatcher was going to drop in on the way to Westminster for a cup of tea and a chat over a garibaldi? I don't think so! Mind you, Diane would have loved that. I'm sure she would have been delighted to sip tea with Mrs Thatcher. I bet she'd ask Maggie how her day went, ask her how tough it was, running the country, and the pair would have had a jolly old time of it. Me, I didn't get so much as a second look! So, just like any other day, I'd head straight upstairs to my bedroom, where I would do my homework, put on my music or write another 'Jessica True' story. Today, I felt like writing, so I threw myself down on my bed, opened up my drawer, slid out my notebook and opened it at the last page I'd written on...

Jessica True is my friend and she is AMAZING! She has long, wavy chestnut brown hair and hazel-green eyes. She has a wonderful, friendly smile and her presence can light up a room. I like to visit Jessica in her home, a place far away from earth. There is no actual sun in Jessica's world but there is always a bright, custardy-yellow glow in the sky. It is the colour of custard creams. In Jessica's world, there are lots of unicorns with pastel pink coats, with sparkly purple flex and light blue horns. And there are also lots of lilac-coloured Pegasuses. Today, Jessica and I ride a Pegasus each. I sit on its back and hold on tight to its mane as it starts to gallop. All of a sudden, it takes off into the air and we are flying. As we fly, I can feel the warmth of the air on my face. It is the best feeling in the world, flying through the custardy sky!

I stopped writing for a second, sucked thoughtfully on the end of my pen and then closed the notepad. All over the front of the pad was Jessica's name written in my best and neatest swirly handwriting. It wasn't so much that she was an imaginary friend – I was too old for that. No, it was just that inside Jessica's world, I was free and everything was lovely. It was a place I could escape to which made me happy. Just writing Jessica's name over and over again made me smile. Now, I started another version: this time I wrote her name inside a curvy pink heart with the words '*Jessica True is a True friend*' studded around the edges.

'AMANDA, COME DOWN NOW, YOUR DINNER IS READY!'

Diane's harsh barking up the stairs disturbed my daydreams. I stopped writing and hurriedly put my notebook back in the drawer. Downstairs, my five-year-old brother was already tucking into his jacket potato and cheese. *Thank God it wasn't that disgusting bean stew again!* I hated the sloppy stew with all the different types of lentils and beans floating around in it: black-eyed beans, butter beans, kidney beans and haricot beans. Who knew there were so many types of beans? It was all for my dad, who had recently turned vegetarian. He said we don't need to eat meat because there isn't any reason to kill animals when there are such lovely alternatives on offer. I wasn't so sure about that but I was pleased he had turned vegetarian because it showed he cared about animals, just like my mum – she loved animals, too.

Diane sat down at the table opposite Terry and started eating. I glanced up at the clock: nearly quarter past five. *Good! That means Dad will be home soon.* He always returned from work at 5.15pm and I liked it when he got home. Today, I couldn't wait to tell him that I'd been picked for the girls' rounders team to play against another local school team after school. I wanted to ask him if I could go before Diane had a chance to say 'no', as she so frequently did. Diane was talking to Terry now, telling him they were off to see Nan and Grandad Seed, her parents, at the weekend.

'Oh, that's a shame! I can't go,' I said. I liked seeing Nan and Grandad Seed and taking their dog Patch for his walk with my brother Terry, but I was due to visit my Chalkley family that weekend.

'Well, it's a court order, you have to go,' Diane replied abruptly. I didn't say anything – that woman loved to state the obvious.

'Hello! Hello, everyone!' Dad called out as he bustled in through the front door. My spirits lifted instantly and I shouted a jolly 'Hello, Dad!' as he pulled his dinner out of the oven and sat down opposite me at the table. We exchanged a quick grin and then he said, 'Cor, this looks good!' before digging in with his fork.

'Terry got a certificate today at school for good Maths work,' Diane announced, as soon as Dad had sat down.

'Wow, well done, Terry!' said Dad through hot mouthfuls of steaming jacket potato. I could tell it was still a bit hot as he juggled the fluffy potato in his mouth. As he blew out his cheeks to cool down the food before swallowing quickly, I giggled.

Then he added: 'You're getting good at doing your sums.'

Terry puffed up proudly.

'The teacher said Terry's ahead of everyone in his class,' Diane went on.

'That's good. Keep it up, son!' Dad nodded, encouragingly.

'Dad, I've been picked for the girls' rounders team...' I couldn't hold back on my own good news any longer.

'Well done, Amanda!' he grinned before shovelling in

another yellow forkful of food. I was about to tell him about playing against another school team when Diane interrupted.

'We're going to see my mum and dad this weekend, David,' she said. 'They said we could all go out for a long walk together with the dog.'

'Can I hold the lead when we take the dog out?' Terry asked eagerly. 'I want to hold the lead, please.'

'Yes. Yes, that will be fine,' said Diane.

By now I had finished my dinner and I got up to get a drink of water from the sink. Then I wandered into the living room, leaving the three of them still chatting away at the table. This wasn't the time to be asking for things, I could tell. Diane was desperate to have her conversation with Dad first. I would have to find another opportunity to bring up the tricky question of the after-school rounders' game.

I'd quickly made some new friends at school – there was Kelly, Annabelle and Zoe – and in the first year, I had such fun with them that I forgot about my work, which meant my grades weren't very good. When it came to giving Dad my report at the end of that first year, I was awkward and nervous but he didn't say anything.

'Dad, did you read my report book?' I asked him later that week.

'Yeah, I read it,' he said distractedly. And that was it. Still, I wanted to do better for myself – I knew I wasn't stupid. My English teacher liked the stories I made up and I always enjoyed Art and PE. But in other areas like Maths and Geography, I lacked confidence – I was never sure if I was doing the work right or getting the correct answers. I agonised over my Maths homework, trying to second-guess myself all the time, tying myself in knots over each question. Dad went to the parents' evenings, but he never told me what they said and that drove me crazy.

'But what did my Geography teacher say about me?' I'd say, trying to wheedle some information out of him the next night.

'Oh, I don't know, Amanda!' Dad rebuffed my efforts. 'Don't worry, you're doing fine. You just need to get a job when you grow up.'

Dad had left school when he was sixteen and gone straight into King's as an engineer, just like his dad. His was a working-class family, none of whom had ever pursued school beyond sixteen. And the way he talked about it, it didn't sound like he had enjoyed his own school years much. Still, I wanted to do well. Early on, I had a sense that education was my key to happiness. I knew that this way I had a chance of making something of myself. And I wanted that very badly. I wanted to prove to myself, to everybody, that I had survived for a reason: there was a reason behind what happened. And secretly, I wanted to make my mum proud.

So at the beginning of my second year at Heathcote, I resolved to work really hard. I got help wherever I could find it, like from my Grandad Frank – he was very clever and always willing to help when I was stuck on my homework. I got my first dictionary as a Christmas present and now I could look up spellings and meanings all by myself. At school, they talked to us about further education a lot, and staying in school and going to university.

That wasn't the kind of talk I got at home.

'You know what you're getting for your sixteenth birthday? A suitcase!'

I think it was meant to be Diane's idea of a joke: a suitcase so that I could leave home and get out from under her feet. I don't know if she expected me to laugh, but I didn't find it very funny – she didn't say it to Terry.

So during the day, I worked hard in school and lost myself in my imaginary worlds at home. Sadly, I couldn't lose myself at night when I was still haunted by night terrors. Now, my brother and I shared a bedroom that was split into two and if I woke up in the night, gripped by terror, I would go over to his bed and snuggle in with him. He didn't mind. It was the only thing I could think of to keep the fear at bay. I was no longer allowed to turn on any lights and Dad and Diane hated it if I woke them up.

One night, Terry half-woke as I jumped into bed beside him.

'What's wrong, Amanda?' he lisped sleepily in his little-boy voice.

'It's nothing. I'm just scared, Terry,' I whispered into his back. 'Go back to sleep.'

'Scared of what?'

'Scared of a man.'

'Who? What man?'

'I don't know...'

And then I heard Terry drifting off beside me, his breathing getting slower and deeper. But I was wide awake. *Who was this man in my dreams?* I was eleven years old now, growing up a little more every day. I didn't want to be like this, scared every night, jumping into bed with my younger brother to chase away the demons in my dreams. *It's so stupid*, I berated myself. I was angry that I was still scared at night, after all these years, and even angrier that I didn't know *what* I was scared of.

So I made a decision.

The next night, when I heard the man's voice, I decided not to run from it or to try and block it out, but to listen. My heart pounded and I felt the prickle of fear creep up the back of my neck. I was numb with terror, but I didn't move or get out of bed. Instead, I kept my eyes shut and I listened. Hard.

Who are you? I want to know! What are you saying?

The voice was indistinct at first, just a vague shouting noise in my head but I listened hard to disentangle the noises from one another. It was hard, like trying to hear one person singing a song while everyone else is shouting during a football match. I had to concentrate very hard to hear. Eventually, my concentration paid off and the voice became clearer: 'Shut up!'

My heart suddenly banged in my chest as I realised who it was: it was *him*! It was the man who had killed my mother.

'Shut up!' he said.

'Shut up and stop crying, or I won't stop!'

'SHUT IT!'

It was *him* and it was the moment he was killing my mum. Now I knew why I had tried to block out his voice for so long, I knew why I had run away: I was terrified of this man, whoever he was. I was frightened of what he was doing to

Mum and terrified of what came next. He was going to come for me. I had seen it, I had been there, and I had felt his strong hands gripping my throat, squeezing all the breath out of me.

But he's not here now, I said to myself. *He's not here. It's just your memory of what happened.* I had to find a way of dealing with it. Now I knew who it was in my head, the fear eased a little. The worst was over: he had already tried to kill me and he hadn't succeeded. This was just the memory of that terrible morning coming back to haunt me, night after night.

Think of something else! I urged myself. *Think of something nice, something good. Quickly!* His voice was getting louder and angrier now. It felt like he was coming closer. The only thing I could think of at that moment was *The Care Bears Movie*. The theme tune was lovely – it was soft and sweet and it was the exact opposite of this voice... so I started to sing in my head: '*Care-a-lot is a place we all can go / Whenever we choose it / Care-a-lot is a feeling we all know / We never do lose it...*'

And suddenly I could hear *my* voice in my head singing and the lovely swirling music that accompanied the song coming in behind me, drowning out the man's shouts. It felt like the music lifted me up to a wonderful place in my dreams, the place where Jessica True lived, a place beyond the clouds, where purple ponies dance in custard-coloured skies:

Yes, I was here – riding on a purple-winged Pegasus, soaring through the skies, free and happy. Now, I was transported up into the sky. Twirling up, up and away, leaving all the sadness and fear down below. Singing this song in my head, I managed to drown out the man's voice and shake off my fear: I was in Care-a-lot and the man was gone. Finally, I had faced my nighttime terror and found a way to beat *his voice*. It had taken years and years, but now I'd found the courage inside myself to beat the memory of that wicked man. I knew after that I would never fear the man's voice again.

I was growing up; I was getting stronger.

CHAPTER 14

A DISCOVERY

My hands trembled as I held the lightweight yellowing newspaper page folded neatly in half. I knew what this was the moment I saw it inside the shoebox: it was something to do with my mum and the attack by the man. I just knew it. The question was: should I look at it? Slowly, I turned the paper over in my hands. I felt myself breathing hard. If I opened it up and looked at this now, there would be no going back. I would find out what had happened to us on the morning of 4 March 1980, and more importantly, who had done it. But was I ready to learn the truth? I was twelve years old now, but I didn't feel like most girls my age. I had lived an interrupted life, one that didn't quite take the ordinary course of childhood. In many ways, I felt much older than twelve.

It was a grey, wet Saturday in November when I went to

stay at Nan Floss's house. We had managed a quick trip to the Lakes in the morning before the rain arrived, but now it was blowing a gale outside and we were trapped indoors without much to do. Nan was downstairs cooking my tea and I had spent the afternoon drawing and writing new 'Jessica True' stories, but after a while I got bored. I wandered upstairs to the back bedroom, where I slept. It had once been Kevin's room but he had moved out a few years earlier. Now it was my clothes that hung in the wardrobe, the set I wore when I was here since I wasn't allowed to bring any of my 'Chalkley family' clothes back home with me.

I sighed and shook my head, thinking about the crazy ongoing feud between the Lowsons and the Chalkleys that seemed to have no end, as I rummaged around in the wardrobe, looking for something to play with – a game, a pack of cards, some books, *anything*! I was desperate.

In the drawers underneath the clothes rail were a few odd bits and pieces left by my Uncle Kevin – some dud batteries, magazines, the remnants of a magic trick and a disposable camera. One by one, I pulled these out, hoping to stumble upon something more exciting, and it was then that I came across the shoebox, stuffed right at the back of one of the drawers. I pulled it out and placed it on the carpet, curious about the contents. The box was very old and battered and when I lifted off the lid, I saw it was filled with pieces of paper and photographs. There were a few photos of my mother, curling up in the corners, and some of her horse sketches too. And then, right at the bottom, there were four old newspaper cuttings, each folded into neat squares. The moment I saw them, I felt butterflies in my stomach. Part of me wanted to put the lid back on the box and shut it away in the drawer forever, forget it was ever there. But another part of me wanted to look.

Was I ready for this? I asked myself again. I knew that if I looked, I would learn something more about my mother's death, about the man who had killed her. Until now he had been a nameless person, in many ways just a phantom haunting my dreams. As I stood holding that piece of folded paper, I knew there was only one way forward; I had to find out. So gently, I started to unfold the paper and I saw it was an old front page of our local paper, the *Stevenage Comet*. The headline at the top of the page was enough to make my heart freeze in my chest:

MURDER CHARGE MAN SAYS 'KINKY SEX GAME GONE WRONG'

Now, there was no turning back. I read on:

Park-keeper John Dickinson told police he killed a young mother when a 'kinky sex session' went wrong.

He claimed attractive Susan Lowson, 25, asked him to tie her up before they had sex at her Stevenage home.

Afterwards he fell asleep and when he woke up she was lying next to him making no sound.

In a statement he said he tried to revive her but failed. He then picked up her lighter and set fire to a piece of paper which he left burning in the bedroom after he left the house...

LIAR! Every inch of my body screamed out the word: LIAR, LIAR, LIAR!

I felt the blood rising to my cheeks and the anger bubbling up inside as I read the article, knowing every word of this man's evidence was a lie. I had been there! He hadn't found her dead. He had killed her – killed her with his own hands! And then he had tried to kill me. My eyes darted around the page and I noticed the date of the article was 3 September 1980 – so they must have caught this man, John Dickinson, quite soon after the fire, I reasoned, and brought him to trial within six months. Now breathing hard and consumed with rage, I read on:

> But Mr Barry Hudson, QC, prosecuting, told St Albans Crown Court yesterday that the Crown believed Dickinson's story was 'entirely untrue'.
>
> Mr Hudson said the fire brigades were called an hour later and found Mrs Lowson's body in the bedroom.
>
> Her four-year-old daughter, Amanda, who was still in the house, was rescued by neighbours. Dickinson, of Lygrave, Broadwater, Stevenage, has denied murdering Mrs Lowson, who was separated from her 22-year-old husband, David. He has also denied arson with intent to endanger Amanda's life.
>
> Full Story – Page 5

With a heavy heart, I picked up the next square of newspaper and unfolded it – page five from the same day's paper. It contained John Dickinson's full, sordid and entirely false account of how my mother had died. Reading his lies and knowing, for the first time, that I was the only person who had seen what had happened was horrible. I was the only witness to my mother's murder and yet I hadn't been asked about it or given evidence at the trial. I suppose I had been too young, too traumatised myself, but for the first time in my life, I felt protective towards my mother. I wanted to defend her, defend her character, and defend her memory from this brute's vicious lies. How dare he! She was innocent in all of this and he made out she was the instigator of some twisted sex game, insisting he tie her up. He claimed he had hit her then as part of their 'fun' but something had gone wrong and she had died accidentally. Also, he claimed he had no idea I was even in the house and had he known, he would never have set fire to the bed.

ARGGHH!! DIRTY, DIRTY LIAR! I screamed silently to myself. It was so enraging. I wanted to turn back time, to return to the trial and tell them all the truth. I wanted them to know what really happened, to clear my mother's name of these nasty lies.

Towards the end of the account given by John Dickinson, the paper quoted Mr Hudson, the prosecutor, who said my mother had died of strangulation. It went on:

He also discounted claims that she had been tied up by saying no marks had been found on her wrists. And he claimed that Dickinson knew about Amanda being in the house. He deliberately set fire to these premises regardless of the safety and welfare of that child.

Worse than that, I thought, *he had tried to kill me!* It occurred to me at that moment that nobody knew. Nobody knew he had strangled me or he would have been tried for attempted murder of me as well as the murder of my mum.

I flipped over the cutting and looked at the back. No, there was nothing more here, so I picked up the fourth cutting. The date was 10 September 1980 and to my great relief, the headline read: MURDERER JAILED FOR LIFE.

The man who tied up, raped and strangled a young mother before setting fire to her house was jailed for life on Friday.

It took a jury at St Albans Crown Court just 40 minutes to find park-keeper John Dickinson guilty of murder and arson.

The court heard that in 1972 he was jailed for three years at Newcastle for three offences of arson after he set fire to his bed-sit in Buchon Street.

This year Dickinson killed attractive Susan Lowson, aged 25, at her home in Colestrete, Stevenage.

He tied her up before raping her and committing other sexual acts.

According to the prosecution, he then strangled her and set fire to the bedroom before leaving the house around 5.30am on March 4.

Mrs Lowson's four-year-old daughter Amanda was trapped in the blazing house and was rescued by milkman Michael Knowles, who kicked the door down and raced up the stairs to grab her.

Sentencing Dickinson, 27, of Lygrave, Stevenage, Mr Justice O'Connor said: 'I pass upon you the sentence required by law and that is life.'

He passed a further life sentence to run concurrently for the arson.

Dickinson, wearing a navy-blue suit and flanked by prison officers, showed no emotion as sentence was passed.

The words went on, but by now my head was swimming and I could barely take it all in. There was so much information and my emotions were all over the place. For a moment, I sat still and closed my eyes, allowing my breathing to come under control. Bit by bit, I allowed myself to think about what I had just found out. The jury hadn't believed him – that was good. I was glad they had taken just forty minutes to find him guilty. And the judge had given him two life sentences. I didn't know how long a life sentence was, but I had a feeling that John Dickinson wasn't getting out of prison anytime soon. This was a relief because just looking at these cuttings made everything so much more real. He was a real man, with a real name and, look, a real face! Now, I feared him terribly. After all, nobody knew he had tried to kill me. Just me. That meant he had a very good reason to come looking for me – to shut me up for good. I shivered at the thought but then told myself not to worry since Dickinson was in prison now and that's where he was likely to stay.

But the things he had said about my mum! I knew they weren't true and yet even the newspaper had repeated the lie that he had tied her up when in the previous cutting, the prosecutor had stated very clearly that there was no evidence she had been tied up. It frustrated me to think that because she had died and was unable to defend her character and reputation, John Dickinson's lies had been allowed to stand. Nobody had challenged his version of things. Even the rebuttals in the paper were small and stuck right at the end of the article, which meant that a person would have to read all the way to the bottom to get to the truth. *And how many people do that?* I wondered. No, people will remember my mum's death as a 'Sex game gone wrong' because that's what the headline had said. It was so unfair.

Slowly, I unfolded the third piece of newspaper: it was a picture of me as a little girl on a space hopper. I was wearing a big grin, cute little bunches and on my legs were the long white surgical socks I recalled having to wear for months after leaving hospital. The headline read: AMANDA IS BOUNCING BACK TO HAPPINESS. The date of the cutting was 11 June 1980 and the article talked about how brave I'd been through all my skin-graft operations. At the very bottom of the piece was just one line: 'A man charged with murdering Mrs Lowson is awaiting trial.' So they had found Dickinson by June, which meant they must have traced him soon after the attack. *What about the milkman*, I wondered. *How had he known I was in the house?* It occurred to me then how brave he had been to come and rescue me. Michael Knowles, I owed my life to that man.

So many thoughts and emotions swirled around my head that day as I carefully refolded all the cuttings and placed them back in the shoebox. Then I put it gently back in the cupboard. Should I tell Floss? I wondered. I felt such a strong need to talk to somebody at this moment, to share all the information I had learned, to work out my feelings at what I had discovered and to learn more. But then I thought about my nan and how much she had suffered at the hands of this man, John Dickinson, losing her daughter and her husband. And I knew I couldn't talk to her about it right now, not in the state I was in. I was so angry and upset, I knew it would only upset her too – and what would be the point of that? No, I needed time to think and absorb everything before I could talk to her calmly. So I went back downstairs as if nothing had happened. Inside, a storm raged but on the outside, I remained silent and calm.

'Nan, I think I'll go for a little walk,' I called to her from the hallway.

'What? Now?' she said, her voice jangling with nerves. She had become very anxious over the years and the smallest thing made her worry. 'But it's still raining!'

'I don't mind, Nan. I fancy a walk. I'm going crazy stuck indoors all day. I think a walk will do me good.'

'Amanda, are you alright?' she asked. 'You don't look so wonderful.'

I snuck a quick peek at myself in the hallway mirror. My face was deathly pale. It gave *me* a shock. So I quickly turned away and pinched my cheeks to bring back the colour.

'Yeah, I'm fine,' I said casually. 'I just need a bit of air, that's all.'

I pulled on my anorak and opened the door. The rain pelted down, blown into horizontal arcs by the fierce wind.

'Do your coat up!' Nan yelled as I threw myself out of the door.

Now I needed to get out, to feel the rain lash against my cheeks. I needed to feel normal, to do something normal to find a way to come to terms with everything I had read.

'Don't worry, Nan!' I called out before slamming the door shut behind me. 'I'll be fine!' And that afternoon, I walked and walked and walked until my legs ached and my feet were wet and sore. I walked up through the Lakes, round and round the park, until the rain stopped and a bright afternoon sun emerged, casting long shadows against the grass.

The pictures, the words and the headlines went over and over in my mind. The big shock was seeing the picture of John Dickinson for the first time – in my dreams, I could never see his face clearly, but now I had a pretty good image in my mind. He had a long, serious face, thin lips and long black wavy hair. I hadn't even known his name until now – he had just been The Murderer, the man who had taken my mum from me. Now that I had a name, a face and an age I suddenly wanted to know a whole lot more. *Who was this man? Why did he choose to kill my mum of all people?* He had committed acts of arson before – I knew that from the cuttings – so why was he free to commit more crimes and what had brought him to my mother's door? It all seemed so strange. In one article it said that John Dickinson claimed he had gone to Mum's house to talk about hiring her room for lodgings and they had ended up kissing and cuddling. I didn't believe that for a second.

From everything I knew about my mother, she was wary of new people, she was shy and she didn't even like to leave the house much. Plus, she was desperately in love with my father. Nan had told me how, after he left, my mum had become reclusive, preferring to stay in the house with me than venture outside. Luckily, Nan lived right around the corner and she would come and visit us a lot. The only place Mum would go was the playground at the Lakes with me. It just didn't seem likely that she would throw herself at the first man who knocked on her door! The more I thought about it, the less sense it made and as the days passed, the questions bubbled up inside me over and over again. *Why us? Why did he attack us?*

Two weeks later, at my nan's house, I plucked up the courage to ask her. We had just finished lunch and she was about to clear the plates when I blurted out: 'Nan, I read something about that man John Dickinson.'

Nan's hand literally stopped in mid-air as she reached for my plate. Then she pulled it back and sat down again, her hands pressed to her chest, as if calming a fluttering heart.

'You read something?' she asked quietly.

'Yes, I found a newspaper cutting from the trial and I was wondering about him.'

Nan nodded slowly.

'I didn't go to the trial,' she said. 'I couldn't stand it. Only Keith went.'

'Nan, did you know who this man John Dickinson was? Do you know why he was in the house?'

Nan took in a deep breath.

'His family lived locally,' she started. 'He came from a nice family, I think they were from Greece originally. We didn't know anything about him going to prison for arson. He and your mother, they were just friends, nothing more. There was never anything between them, not like it said in the paper. This is a community area, everyone knows everyone. He worked in the park. Anyway, from what I can make out he went to your mother because he needed somewhere to stay after his wife kicked him out. She had a spare room she was thinking of renting out to bring in a bit of extra money. Your mother might have felt sorry for him and let him in.'

Nan stopped then and sighed: 'His family moved away after the trial. This community is too small – it was too hard for them.'

I sat quietly for a minute, thinking about what Nan had told me. It was true my mother was kind-hearted and she might have felt sorry for John Dickinson. But would she have asked him to stay over the night? Possibly, but only as a friend, on the couch downstairs. So why did he attack her? Was it because she refused to sleep with him? Or had he planned it all along?

'Why?' I said out loud. 'Why do you think he chose us? Why did he kill Mum?'

'Oh, Amanda, I don't know!' Nan shook her head, tears welling up. 'Who knows why that madman did what he did? Maybe he saw your mother was on her own and he thought he could worm his way into her life and when that didn't work, he lost the plot. I don't know! But I tell you one thing: she never did any of those perverted things he said in the trial. He lied his head off!'

146

Above: Horse crazy: Mum loved to ride her horse Sherry to the shops.

Below: Mum Susan and Dad David on their wedding day with all their guests.
From left to right: Uncle Billy (Nan Flo's brother), Geoff (Dad's best man),
Grandad Frank, Nan Eve, Uncle Kevin, Dad, Mum, cousin Greg, Nan Flo,
Marion (Geoff's wife), Aunty Carol, Uncle Mick, cousin Claire, Grandad Bill.

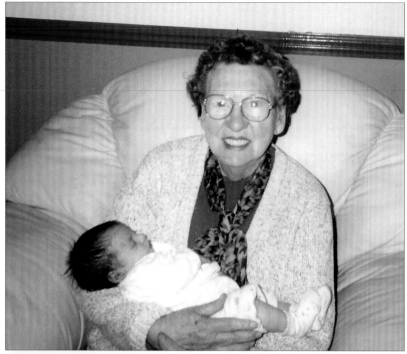

Above: My beloved Nan Flo with my daughter, her great-granddaughter Susanna, named after my mum.

Below left: A family photo – Dad with me as a toddler, my mum Sue and my cousin Greg.

Below right: Happy by the seaside – Mum on the beach on a day trip to Caister in Norfolk.

Above left: My mother's daughter: me at nineteen years old.

Above right: A cherished photo of me and Mum on top of the slide at the Lakes. Through the years I've kept it in a frame on my bedside table. Though it is faded now, it still makes me smile.

Below left: My mum Sue looking radiant.

Below right: Wedded bliss: I was so happy when I got married to Glen and Mum was a big part of our special day.

Above left: My Mum's older brother Keith with my husband Glen at the christening of a family friend's daughter. I was touched to be asked to be her Godmother.

Above right: A proud day: graduating with a First in Educational Studies with my family at my side.

Below: Becoming a mum has fulfilled me in so many ways: Glen, myself and our daughters Susanna and Isabelle enjoying an Italian meal for Glen's birthday.

'Yeah, I know that, Nan,' I replied, pleased that she felt the same way as me. 'I know he did it deliberately. I know he set out to harm us – I just can't work out why. I mean, what did we do to him?'

Nan sighed.

'You can't put yourself into the head of a madman,' she said dully. 'All I know is that my Sue was a kind, loving person and she would have taken pity on him. She was soft, your mum. And who knows, maybe she was a bit lonely because she wasn't getting out so much back then. She invited him in, just for a bit of company and then... and then... then he went and done that to her! I feel sick just thinking about it, thinking about what she went through.'

We left it at that. I didn't talk to anyone else about it because I knew they all had their different ideas. The problem was that John Dickinson's behaviour was so far from the sphere of normal human behaviour it was impossible to see any reason or rationale behind it. That frightened me all the more – I mean, how could I protect myself from a psychotic killer? If Dickinson got out of prison and decided to kill me, how could I stop him? I wouldn't even recognise him if he walked past me in the street. I started to shiver. He could be walking past me right now, looking right at me, and I wouldn't even know.

I was no longer afraid of a nameless, faceless bogeyman, stalking my nightmares. Now, I was afraid of a living, breathing person called John Dickinson, who had every reason to hunt me down and kill me. Thank God I had never told anyone what he had done to me that day; thank God I had kept my mouth shut! Now, I had more reason than ever not to reveal to people that he had tried to strangle me to death.

Was I destined to die young, just like my mother, at the hands of the very same murderer?

CHAPTER 15

TRUE
COLOURS

An awkward silence filled the room. Some of the kids near to me shifted uncomfortably in their seats. I looked straight down at the blank paper on my desk and felt my cheeks grow hot.

How could she do this to me? Was she really that insensitive?

Just a few moments ago, our form teacher, Miss Revel, had set the whole class a writing assignment.

'You are to write a story,' she started, 'and the theme is that you are in your home when a fire breaks out. Tell me what happens. How do you feel? Does anyone get burnt or even die in the fire? What happens next?'

No one had moved after she had delivered this instruction. In fact, at that moment it felt like all the air had been sucked out of the room and everyone was looking at me. I couldn't bear to raise my eyes. *Didn't she know?* I wondered. *What am I going to do?* I felt my breathing coming in shaky starts now and resolved at that moment that whatever happened, I wouldn't write down my real experiences but instead make up a fantasy story. If she wanted me to share my darkest, most painful memories, she had a bloody strange way of going about it! I felt a surge of anger rise up in my throat but I couldn't speak, I could barely breathe.

'Yes, Mark?' said Miss Revel. The silence was broken. One of the boys at the back had raised his hand.

'Erm, Miss, what if you've had a similar experience to this one you've outlined? I mean, you wouldn't want to think about it, would you?'

'Maybe not,' replied Miss Revel, shrugging. She didn't seem to get what Mark was hinting at, but of course he was talking about me. A sensitive suggestion instantly dismissed.

Another voice near to me spoke, one of the girls: 'This isn't right, Miss. Let's do the story about something else, something different. Just not a house fire, okay?'

I looked up, astonished by the outburst. The girl's name was Dawn and although we had been in the same class for nearly three years now, we weren't in the same group of friends. She didn't even know me that well, yet she was sticking up for me. I felt a little wave of gratitude for her thoughtful idea.

'No, look, come on!' Miss Revel objected. 'This is the theme and all you have to do is write a little story from your imagination. So let's get going, shall we?'

Still, nobody moved. In the whole class of thirty children, not one person picked up a pen. *They all knew.* Every single one of my classmates knew about my background. Still, I just sat there, my head bowed, feeling uncomfortable and strangely exposed.

Finally, Mark broke the stand-off.

'No, I'm not doing it!' he said, shaking his head and folding his arms. 'You can't make me.'

'Me neither,' said the boy next to him.

'Nor me.'

'I'm not doing it either.'

'This is wrong.'

'I won't write that type of story.'

The room was filled with the voices of rebellion. I looked around, gobsmacked, as the whole class, as one, stuck up for me and refused to write the story that they all knew would cause me pain and trauma. Carefully, I let out a quiet sigh and in that moment felt overwhelmed with gratitude. I knew that Miss Revel couldn't make everyone do it. Well, she could try, but it wasn't like this was an exam. What would be the point? I looked up briefly and shared a fleeting smile with a couple of my classmates. Here they were, just ordinary kids – usually goofing and clowning around – and yet, when it came down to it, they showed their true colours: caring, brave and strong. They had thrown a protective ring around me and I felt safe among them all.

For a moment, Miss Revel just sat on the edge of her desk, her arms folded over her chest, scowling at the whole class. But it was useless: she knew she had lost this battle.

'Oh, all right!' she finally exploded, throwing her arms up in resignation. 'Suit yourselves. Get your books out, you can read until the bell goes.'

And so that is what we did. And as soon as we were released from the class, I bolted out of my seat and towards the door, head down. I couldn't bear to talk to anyone about what had just happened or even look anyone in the eye. For the rest of the day, I was shaken up. *Miss Revel – did she really not know?* She acted like this was no big deal so it made me think that maybe she had set us this task completely ignorant of the fact that I had lost my mother in the exact scenario she had outlined. But then something in my gut told me she must have known because she didn't appear surprised by Mark's objection. *So what was her motivation? Did she want me to open up to her?* If it was a twisted ploy, it was one that was clearly never going to work. All I knew was that I felt incredibly grateful to my classmates for standing up for me.

At thirteen, I was a sporty and slender girl and had started a paper round to earn a little bit of money to buy my own toiletries. I had asked my dad and Diane for pocket money but they had refused, suggesting that if I wanted my own income, I should earn it. A paper round was the only way I could do this until I got to fourteen, so every morning I was up at 6am to get to the shop for 6.30am. I didn't have a bike like a lot of the other boys – and it was mostly boys – so I had to take my heavy bag of papers on foot, and at first the large shoulder bag really hurt. Of course it got lighter as I completed my round. My route started at one end of The Paddocks, went down the road and then a few little roads off the main road. Usually, after I completed my round, I'd pop into Nan's for a cup of tea and a bite to eat before heading to school by 8.45am.

By now Diane didn't mind that I went to my nan's for some breakfast. It was preferable to me coming back home and ringing the doorbell each morning.

'Why can't I just have my own key?' I asked, for what seemed like the hundredth time. It didn't make any sense to me – after school every day I'd have to ring my own doorbell like a stranger, waiting for Diane to let me in. I had been walking to school and back on my own since I was six years old and still, seven years later, I didn't have my own front door key. It was as if they didn't trust me, but I was never told *why*. And now that Diane had a variety of cleaning jobs it made things even more difficult. Most days after school now, Terry and me went round to Nan Eve's house until either my dad or Diane returned home. Fortunately, I didn't have to ring the doorbell to Nan Eve's house – she had given me a key to her house years before, so I just let myself in once I had finished my paper round. It struck me as funny that I had a key to her house but not one to my own. Every afternoon and morning, seven days a week, I did my paper round which earned me £10.80 a week, enough to buy myself all my own toiletries and the occasional treat.

One day, not long after I turned fourteen, my Aunty Sue, my Uncle Kevin's girlfriend, said she had something for me. It was her bike – she said she didn't need it anymore as she had a car now to get to work. I was so thrilled, I nearly screamed.

Most kids my age had had a bike for a good few years already, so if they went on bike rides, I always had to borrow somebody else's and that felt a bit awkward. I didn't even know how to ride one until a couple of years before when

Aunty Carol taught me in her back garden. There wasn't that much room so we had to keep going round and round in circles, but she never gave up.

'That's it,' she encouraged. 'Keep peddling! Keep peddling!'

I peddled like mad and eventually, after a good few wobbles and a couple of tumbles, I found I was doing it on my own. Having my own bike made my paper round so much easier – and quicker! Now, I found I could complete the whole round in just under twenty minutes. One afternoon, I dashed back home after school to start my round but my bike, which I had left in the garden, leaning up against the back wall of the house, was nowhere to be seen. Puzzled, I looked around, thinking maybe Diane had moved it while I was at school but no, it was gone. Completely gone. *Oh, no! Had it been stolen?* I was panicked at the thought of my bike being taken from me so soon after getting it.

'Diane, have you see my bike?' I asked anxiously, wandering into the house.

'Your bike?' Diane was on her knees by the washing machine, sorting out a basketful of laundry. 'I think Caroline's got it.'

'Caroline?' this was the little sister of a friend of mine, one of our neighbours. 'Why would Caroline have it?'

'Oh, she asked to borrow it, so I gave it to her.'

This was very strange. I walked over to Caroline's house, across the green, and immediately saw her whizzing up and down the street on my bike, *my new bike*.

'Caroline – can I have my bike back, please?' I called out. Caroline was ten years old but already she could ride really well and she came skidding to a halt next to me, putting her foot down on the floor to steady herself.

'But it's mine,' she said, breathlessly.

'What do you mean? It's not yours. It's *mine*. Give it back!' I was quite angry now.

'But I was told by your stepmum I could keep the bike.'

'No, you can't keep it. You need to give me back my bike – I need it. Anyway, whatever Diane says it's not her bike, it's mine.'

Caroline shrugged and threw her leg over one side of my blue-and-white bike then pushed the handlebars towards me. From the way she gave up the bike so easily, it was clear none of this had been her idea. She never planned to take my bike away from me. I knew she was telling the truth. Diane had simply given it to her – for keeps! I was hopping mad, but there was no time. I had to get to the shop to pick up my paper bag straight away or I could get into trouble and lose my job. So I threw my leg over the bike and sped away, all the while fuming.

Later, when Diane opened the door to me, I stood on the doorstep, frowning, clearly holding the bike she had been so keen to get rid of. I was determined to have my say.

'Diane, this is *my* bike,' I said, my voice quivering with a mixture of anger, fear and frustration. 'You can't go giving it away. It's not yours to give away.'

She just raised an eyebrow at me, turned and walked indoors without saying a word. I wanted to shout out after her, to make her stop and demand an answer: *Why would you do that? Why would you give my bike away like that?* But what would be the point? She didn't care enough to give me an answer and anyway, in my heart, I knew the answer for myself. Deep down, I knew what she thought of me and now our relationship became even more strained and uncomfortable.

Now that I was fourteen, I could have a real part-time job, so I started working on the tills of the Co-op on Saturdays. It was great to have my own money and a bit of independence. By now I was working two jobs plus doing all of my schoolwork – it was tiring, but I didn't mind and at least it got me out of the house. Occasionally, I bought myself some clothes and one day I found a cute little denim mini-skirt in Topshop, which I loved. Until now I hadn't worn shorts or skirts that much. I was a bit of a tomboy and wore jeans most of the time, but now that I was getting older, I wanted to wear more girly clothes, like skirts. Only I felt self-conscious about my legs. Despite the fact that all my family had told me that my scars were healing nicely, there had come a moment when I realised they were never going to fade completely: this was scar tissue and it was here to stay.

'Can you see the scars, Nan?' I asked my Nan Floss that weekend when I tried on my new denim mini. I was due to meet a couple of friends at the McDonald's in town at midday and wanted to wear my new skirt, but when I looked in the mirror, all I could see were the white patches on my legs.

Nan stood behind me, and we both stared at my legs in the mirror.

'They look fine to me but I'm sure we can find you something to cover them up, if they make you feel uncomfortable,' she said, biting one of her fingers. 'What about tights?'

'I don't want to wear tights, Nan. Nobody wears tights with a skirt like this – besides, I'd be too hot.'

'All right, well, let's see what we can find. I think I saw an advert in a magazine for some cream that might do the trick. I'll send off for it and then next time you come round, you can wear the skirt and use the cream to cover up the scars.'

The following week I was so excited to get to Nan's house. I'd been thinking about the special cream all week and how it would help me to be able to wear shorts and skirts in the summer. As soon as I got to Nan's I asked her if she had got it and she nodded. She bustled out of the room and returned with a large tub in her hand. 'Camouflage Cream' read the label on the tub.

I could hardly wait to get upstairs and put it on. Now I could be like all my friends and wear little skirts all summer! In my room, I took off my jeans and read the instructions – the cream was a bit like face foundation but much thicker and heavier. I think it was meant to be the same colour as my skin but it was darker than the skin on my legs. I suppose this was inevitable since my legs were always covered up and didn't get to see the sun that often. I smeared the cream up and down my legs, trying to smooth in the bits where my scars met my normal skin, blending it just as the instructions said, to give a 'natural' look.

Then I slipped on my new denim skirt and slid my feet into my special 'going out' heels – they weren't big heels but they were the first ones I'd ever had and I wasn't allowed to wear them at home so I kept them at Nan's house.

Taking one last look in the mirror, I eyed my legs in the new cream. *Not bad*, I thought. From this distance, you couldn't see the scars at all.

'All ready?' Nan asked, grinning from the hallway.

'Yup!'

'You look super, sweetheart,' she said, giving me a quick peck on the cheek. 'Go on! Go out and have a good time with your pals.'

I flung open the front door and happily tripped down the steps on the garden path. At that moment, my legs were bathed in bright sunlight and for the first time, I got to see the full effect of the cream in the daylight.

Oh my God, they looked hideous! Great big globs of dark cream were smeared up and down my legs like I'd just got out of a bath full of mud.

I can't go out looking like this. No way! I'll give people nightmares!

Quickly, I spun around and ran back up the stairs, two at a time, then banged urgently on the front door. Nan was amazed to see me back again so soon.

'Quick, let me in!' I shrieked. 'No one can see me like this!'

She pulled open the door and I flew up the stairs. In the bathroom I cleaned and scrubbed away at my legs until all the nasty foundation was gone. Then I patted my legs dry and put my old jeans back on. Phew! That was better. I went downstairs.

'No good?' Nan looked up from where she was sat on the sofa watching TV. She looked a little sad. Poor Nan, she was only trying to help. I leaned down and hugged her round the neck.

'Nah,' I whispered into her ear, 'I looked like the creature from the Black Lagoon!' She chuckled and I went on: 'I think it probably looks better natural, with nothing on. But thanks anyway, Nan – you know, for getting the cream. I appreciate it.'

Nan lifted her hand and patted at my arms around her neck. I bent my head towards hers so that our foreheads touched.

'I just want you to be happy, Amanda. You know that.'

'I know, Nan.'

One morning, a couple of weeks later, I woke up with a feeling like my head was about to explode. Every cell in my body ached and I was sweating madly but freezing at the same time.

'Come on, Amanda!' Diane put her head round my bedroom door. 'Get up, time for school!'

'I can't,' I croaked feebly from under my duvet. 'I'm ill.'

Diane frowned for a moment then barked: 'No, you're not! Come on, get up. You're going in whether you like it or not.'

Then she disappeared.

I closed my eyes and sighed. All I wanted was to stay right here under the covers and sleep off this sickness, which seemed to have me pinned to the mattress. I could barely lift my head off the pillow let alone pick up my whole body and drag myself into lessons. *What was wrong with that woman?* It's not as if she had even looked at me properly, let alone taken my temperature or felt my forehead. I knew I was ill. It wasn't like I was throwing a sickie; I would never do that! I actually *liked* going to school – it was infinitely preferable to being at home – so I would never avoid it, if I could help it. But today... today, I honestly felt like I'd been hit by a truck.

'Come *on*!' Diane yelled from downstairs. 'Up, up, *up*!'

'Diane, I'm not well!' I yelled back. Ouch! That hurt my throat. I swallowed and again winced in pain.

Who had crawled into my throat and filled it full of razor blades?

'Five minutes!' came her response. 'You've got five minutes till you have to get out of this house.'

Urgh! It was hopeless. Diane never backed down; she never, ever changed her mind. Once she had decided, that was it. She didn't like me being in the house on my own. Because she was leaving, it meant I had to go too, illness or no illness.

Somehow I managed to throw on my uniform and then half-stumbled, half-fell out of the front door. Diane slammed it shut behind me, got in her car and drove off, never giving me a second look. If she had, she might have seen how ill I was.

Stuff this! I thought.

There was no way I could make it through a day at school, so instead, I walked to the doctor's surgery – an epic struggle up the road, which might well have been the other side of the earth. Every step took superhuman effort and halfway through, I had to stop and lean against the wall, fearing I might throw up. Once the receptionist saw my grey, sweaty skin, she ushered me straight in to see my GP.

He took my temperature and listened to my chest.

'Looks like you've got tonsillitis,' he said brusquely, before writing me out a prescription for penicillin. 'Pick this up from the pharmacy and then I think it's bed rest for you for at least three or four days. No school this week!'

I was grateful to him, not least because he actually confirmed that I wasn't well. And also, he didn't ask why I was there on my own. Had he asked me where my parents were, I think I might have cried, right there in his office.

Exhausted, I dragged myself from the surgery to my Nan Eve's door, fumbling in my pockets to find my front-door key. With the very last ounce of energy I had left, I managed to put the key in the lock and turn. Then I fell in the front door and weakly called out: 'Nan!'

Nan came running out to the corridor and when she saw the state of me, she put my arm around her shoulder and called out for Grandad to come and help.

'Grab her other arm,' she said. 'Come on, darling. Let's get you over to the sofa.'

Right then, I felt overwhelming gratitude towards my grandparents as they carried me to the sofa in their living room. There, I collapsed and a minute later, Nan Eve threw a blanket over me. Almost immediately, I closed my eyes and fell into a deep, dreamless sleep.

Later, Nan woke me up to give me a sip of water and my medicine. I refused the toast she offered, but took a couple of spoons of warm tomato soup before falling back to sleep. The next time I woke up, Nan was on the phone. I could tell by the way she was speaking that my dad was on the other end.

'No, she's not well,' she spoke tartly. This was Nan's angry voice. 'She's got tonsillitis. She hasn't moved off the sofa all day, she's hot and clammy, and she's got a temperature. I don't know how, but she managed to get some penicillin from her doctor before she got here. But really, David, she shouldn't be *here* at all!'

Silence.

'Well, I don't know, David, but don't you think she should be at *home?* In bed?'

Silence again.

'Alright, fine. We'll see you soon then.'

Dad came to pick me up in the car that night and after carrying me into the house, he put me to bed. I stayed there for the next three days until the fever finally broke and I started to feel more like myself again. Gradually, my strength returned and after a week off school, I was finally well enough to go back.

But one thing never recovered: any good feeling I had towards Diane. The uncaring and unsympathetic way she had turfed me out of the house when I was sick hardened my heart towards her. She would never like me, she would never have any feelings towards me, and there was absolutely nothing I could do about it. Just like my classmates, when it really mattered, Diane had shown her true colours. I knew our relationship would never recover, but I never imagined for one moment that things would get as bad as they did.

CHAPTER 16

THE
HOME FRONT

'You know what you're getting for your sixteenth birthday?' Diane sneered at me. 'Suitcases! So you can pack your stuff and bugger off out of here!'

With that, she threw back her head and guffawed, as if she'd just cracked the funniest joke in the world. But if it was a joke, it wasn't funny, and it certainly wasn't amusing the hundredth time I heard it. Fifteen years old now and just a month away from my sixteenth birthday, I rolled my eyes and sighed. More importantly, it was GSCE year for me, a big year! I was taking eight GCSEs – English, Maths, History, Drama, Geography, Science, BTC (computers) and Humanities. It was a lot of work and I tried really hard to get good grades in all my coursework, but while some subjects came easily to me, like English, Humanities and History, I really struggled with the maths and science subjects. In exams, I got confused easily and never trusted my own answers, so I had to work hard to keep my panic under control and answer the questions one by one without getting stuck.

The fact is I wanted to go on and study for my A-levels. I knew that my best chance of making a good life for myself was through education and if I could get my qualifications, then I could get a good job. I wanted to make something of myself; in my heart I knew I wanted to make Mum proud. But of course Diane had other ideas. To her mind, my reaching sixteen years of age meant one thing: moving out. I didn't know how to break the news to her, so I talked to Dad first.

'What do you want to do A-levels for?' he asked, bemused, when I told him about my plans. 'You just need to do alright in your exams and then get a job.'

'Dad!' I sighed, exasperated. He and Diane seemed to belong to another era, a time when everyone walked out of school at sixteen and straight into the working week.

'It's not like that anymore,' I explained. 'You can't just walk into any job you want with GCSEs. Everyone has to get better qualifications these days to get the good jobs.'

'Oh yes, and what job are you planning to do, then?'

I was glad he had asked me this.

'Right, well, I've been talking to the school and they've worked out a whole plan for me. They say if I do well and pass my GCSEs, I can do A-level Drama and Sociology, and after that, I could take a BTec in Childcare. That's what I want to do. I'd really like to work with children one day, Dad.'

'Well, that sounds like a lot of studying, Amanda,' Dad frowned, scratching the day-old stubble on his chin. I could tell he was thinking the same thing as me: Diane. Of course she wouldn't like it. She had her own ideas for me after my GCSEs – those *bloody* suitcases – and she wouldn't like me staying on at school. That was why I was telling Dad now, before I took my exams – just so he could speak to Diane about it, to try and get her to agree.

'I can do it, Dad,' I said quietly. 'If you give me the chance, I promise I can do it.'

April came and went – there wasn't much fuss made about my sixteenth birthday. To my great relief, the suitcases never materialised, but I hardly felt welcome in my own home. It was as if I was a hindrance to my stepmum and so, if I wasn't out working – I had taken on a new Sunday job in Toys R Us – I spent most of my time in my room, studying or listening to my music. In May I took my exams and to my great relief, I landed a handful of Bs, Cs and Ds – enough to get me onto the A-level courses I wanted. I was thrilled. My Nan Eve and Grandad Frank were really proud of me too, as were the whole of my Chalkley family.

But shortly after my results, I was at home in the living room with Diane and Dad when she announced that if I was planning on staying at home from now on, I had to pay money for my rent, food and utility bills.

'These things aren't free, you know,' she said pointedly. 'Your father and I work hard to pay the bills. To pay for *you*! I think five pounds a week would be fair.'

'But I'll be studying full-time, doing my A-levels,' I pointed out. I only earned £7.50 a week total from my Sunday job. If I gave away a fiver, that would leave me with just £2.50 to buy everything I needed.

'How can I earn enough money to pay rent if I'm studying?' I asked. It didn't seem fair. 'I can pay you a little, I suppose. Maybe £1 a week?'

But Diane was resolute: 'If you're not going to pay your way, I don't see why we have to feed you. Or do your laundry for that matter. You can buy your own food from now on, and do your own bloody laundry too!'

I was gobsmacked. As my friends and I started our A-levels, I found that all the money I earned from my part-time job went towards buying food, Tampax, toiletries and washing powder. At nights, I'd find myself scrubbing my clothes by hand in the sink, hanging them over the radiators to dry. I wasn't allowed into the kitchen and I was barred from the fridge so I'd buy ready-made sandwiches from the corner shop and eat them on my bed. Late at night, I'd sit in my room and cry. I felt completely disconnected from the people who were supposed to be my parents, looking after me. *How dare she ask me to call her a mother!* I raged inside. *What sort of a mother makes it so difficult for a child to study, to better herself?* I looked out of the window and shook my head. *How had it come to this? Oh, Mum, I wish you were here now! All I want to do is get on with my life and do well. How can this be happening?* I didn't understand it. We weren't poor – Dad and Diane both worked, plus, they were still getting child benefit for me. How could they refuse to feed me?

One night, sick of the situation, I took Dad to one side while Diane was out of the room and asked: 'What's going on here? Diane won't feed me. Is that all right with you, Dad? Are you okay with that?'

I couldn't understand how he could allow himself to go along with this. I was his daughter. If anyone had a duty to look after me it was him. But Dad had never stood up to Diane before and he certainly wasn't going to start now.

'You can go and eat at your nan's house,' he suggested. 'She'll give you food, if you ask her.'

'But I can't even get into my own house when I need to!' I said.

'Here,' he said, digging into his pocket, 'I've got a spare key. You can use this to get in and out of the house but shush' – he put a finger to his lips – 'not a word to Diane, right? This is our little secret.'

I took the key reluctantly. Finally, aged sixteen, I was getting a front-door key, but not openly. I had to sneak around behind Diane's back.

So now began a silent war, a battle of wills: me, just trying to survive while Diane tried to make my life as hard as possible. I think this was her way to get me out of the house – if she made my life impossible then I might just up and leave of my own account. And it wasn't always a silent war either. Sometimes she'd come into my room and make snarky little comments just to try and wind me up.

'You're wasting your time studying,' she'd sneer at me from the doorway. 'Why don't you just go out and get a full-time job? We don't want you here!'

At times the comments got nasty, and she called me a 'useless, lazy bitch' and then she'd twist the knife in by saying that

I would never amount to much. I tried not to rise to it, not to give her the satisfaction of seeing that she had upset me. Instead, I did my best to avoid her, sneaking into the house when she wasn't home to make myself a little sandwich or to do my washing. It didn't always work. One time I left my damp hand-washed clothes hanging over the radiator in the bathroom. When I came home, those wet clothes were all in a crumpled heap on my bedroom floor. Apparently, I wasn't even allowed to use the bathroom rail now!

Just as Dad said, Nan Eve fed me if I turned up, but I felt bad about imposing myself on her. I tried not to complain to anyone, and I certainly didn't need to give my Chalkley family any further ammunition against the Lowsons, but I couldn't hide it forever and gradually, they learned what was going on.

'She can't do that, surely!' Nan Floss said. 'She has to feed you. Can't we do something, dear?'

'I honestly don't know what's to be done,' I sighed.

It was now the New Year and I was getting on quite well with my A-levels but the stress of my home life was beginning to affect my studies. It was hard to concentrate for any length of time and I found the easiest place to study was in the library at school, which meant most of the time I was out of the house and only really went home to sleep.

'Well, you know you can come here anytime, don't you?'

'Yeah, thanks, Nan,' I smiled weakly. I felt like a hopeless charity case.

I was still paying Diane £1 a week, which meant I had to work quite hard to ensure I had enough money to give her as well as support myself, so I picked up any little odd jobs I could. Usually I babysat for my cousin Greg's girlfriend Jackie once or twice a week. She had a lovely little girl called Zoe, but even that wasn't hassle-free! Diane always insisted I was home by midnight and one night, Jackie wasn't home in time.

I called home five minutes before I was due back.

'Jackie's not back yet,' I said. 'I can't leave.'

'I don't care,' Diane snapped. 'You need to get back here now!'

'What am I supposed to do…?' But the phone clicked off. She had hung up. I stood there, holding the phone in my hands and looking at it, baffled. Did she really expect me to leave a three-year-old child alone in the house? The clock struck midnight. *What am I, bloody Cinderella?* There was nothing else for it – I had to bring the little girl back home with me or I knew Diane would lock the door and I wouldn't actually be able to get home myself.

So at ten past twelve, I gently woke Zoe and bundled her into her thick coat, confused and bleary-eyed from sleep. Quietly, I cajoled her into her buggy and then bent down to strap her in. Thankfully, just as I was about to wheel her outside, Jackie made her apologies: 'Sorry 'bout that, 'Manda, love, got a bit carried away… Enjoying myself a bit too much. Ha, ha, ha!' she laughed. She looked down now and noticed Zoe staring back up at her. 'Everything alright here?' she asked.

'Erm, yeah, fine,' I said. 'But Diane said I had to get home so that's why I've got the buggy out. Sorry, I'll put her back to bed. I didn't really know what to do…'

'Mmmm… okay. S'fine. How much do I owe you?'

I thought she would be hopping mad at me for having her

little girl up and out of bed at midnight. But it was a close call – things were getting out of hand.

'She did *what*?' Nan Floss could hardly believe her ears.

'Snatched it right out of my hand,' I repeated.

'The sandwich?'

'Yup!'

I could hardly believe it myself. A week later, and I was recounting Diane's latest outrage to my sympathetic Nan. When I first started telling Floss about Diane catching me in the kitchen making myself a cheese sandwich, I had thought it was a funny story. I always tried to look on the bright side and I thought it would amuse her to hear how Diane had literally grabbed the sandwich out of my hands. It was so ridiculous! But as I was telling her, I realised there was nothing funny about this at all and I felt the familiar prickle of tears sting my eyes. This was too stressful; it was too much for me to cope with. I'd put on a brave face for too long now. Finally, I had to face the truth: life at home had become unbearable. I burst into tears.

'Oh, Amanda!' Nan enveloped me in a big hug. 'We've got to do something about this, love. It can't go on. What about social services? I mean, you're a ward of court. Why don't we talk to them and ask them to help?'

Nan called the social services on my behalf and requested the meeting at her home the following week, the last week in April 1992. It felt like the safest place to talk to them. I got there half an hour before the lady arrived. She seemed friendly, professional and wore a smart blue suit. We all sat down together in the living room and almost before we began, I started to cry.

'I just had to do something,' I explained. 'I'm at the end of my tether. It's my stepmum, Diane – she's making life really hard for me. I'm not even allowed my own key! She doesn't want me in the house on my own, so if they're not in, I have to wander the streets or go to my nan's house. She doesn't do my laundry and says I have to pay her rent. She doesn't see why she has to feed me and so I have to buy all my own food.'

It all came tumbling out of me. The lady nodded sympathetically, her head cocked to one side, as she wrote it all down. All the while, Nan Floss held my hand.

After I'd told her everything I said: 'What can be done? I really want to do my A-levels. I feel this is unjust.'

'What if we speak to your dad and Diane?'

'Yeah...' I shrugged. 'I suppose. You could try.'

'The alternative is for you to move out. To try and get supported accommodation if you feel that living at home has become untenable.'

I nodded, silently this time. It was such a big thing to move out – how could I move out, support myself and carry on my A-levels?

'Will I still be able to study?' I asked the social worker.

'It might be tricky. Let's start by talking to your dad, shall we?'

Every day for the next two weeks I scanned the post, hoping to see a letter from social services to Dad, but nothing. And he never mentioned that they had been in touch. By now the *silent* part of the war with Diane was over and it was full-on hostilities. She had taken to barging into my room to make nasty comments about me, just trying to provoke a reaction. She called me names and even mentioned my mum, which really upset me. After one particularly hurtful outburst, she slammed my door and I immediately burst into tears. She had called Mum a horrible name and I was so upset, I just sobbed and sobbed.

Five minutes later, there was a tentative knock on the door.

'Amanda?' Dad said my name as he opened the door. Quickly, I turned my face away and gulped back the tears, swiping at my face with the back of my sleeve. I didn't want him to see me like this, a snotty, horrible mess.

He stood there in the doorway, not moving.

'Are you okay, Amanda?' he asked gently.

I didn't reply. Inside, I was raging.

He could see for himself that I was very far from okay, so what was the point in even saying it? He *knew*! He knew very well how horrible she was to me and yet not once did he stand up for me. I had given up on my dad now: he knew what was happening and he was the only person who could do something about it.

'Go away, Dad!' I said quietly and a second later, I heard the door click shut.

The next day I went to my mother's graveside with my Nan Floss. We took a lovely bunch of pink and yellow roses and carnations. I just needed to feel close to Mum, to feel that she was with me. As I sat down on the ground beside her grave, I felt the warm sun on my skin. I let the tears fall freely now as I spoke silently to her.

Oh, Mum, I wish you were here now. How different my life would be if you were still alive. I just don't know how much more of this I can take...

CHAPTER 17

FIGHTING BACK

'Get up! Come on, get up! Get out of the house. You're going out *now*!'

My eyes opened slowly. Groggy and unrested, I looked over to my alarm clock – the time read 8am. I heard my brother in the bathroom, getting ready for school.

'I don't have a class till ten,' I croaked at Diane, who stood in my doorway, arms folded, her face screwed up with annoyance and distaste, as if she'd just eaten something really disgusting. What a sight to wake up to! But this morning I felt really tired and I knew that I could use an extra hour in bed.

'Don't argue!' Diane snapped. 'You've got to get up because I'm going out now.' And with that, she stormed out of the room.

It was early May, just a couple of weeks after my seventeenth birthday, and this morning I struggled to get motivated while Diane bustled about the house, fizzing with ill-temper.

'Come on, you lazy cow!' she yelled from downstairs just as I was brushing my teeth. I was so sick of this. It's not like I was ever given any warning; it's not like she told me the night before that she wanted me out of the house early the next day. No, there was never any warning. It was all a surprise to me, so I had no time to prepare.

'Why do you need me to leave?' I shouted back down at her. I'd worked and earned my own money since the age of thirteen, I babysat other people's children, I got my GCSEs and I was working hard to stay in school and I'd never done anything to get me into trouble. I just couldn't understand what I'd done to make her think I was untrustworthy. Why couldn't I spend one bloody hour in the house alone?

'I told you already. Don't argue with me, you useless child! Just get your lazy arse out of my house!'

Fuming, I pulled on my jeans and slipped into a pair of trainers. Then I gathered up my school bag and all the things I needed for that day. I was too rushed – I needed more time.

'Out *now*!' Diane ordered and I raced down the stairs, nearly tripping up over my coat and bag as I went. She led me out the back way, then closed the door behind us.

'Why can't...' I started.

'Just stop your bloody moaning!' she exploded. 'Always moaning and whining. Just like your mother: a fucking slag! And that's what you are too – a slag!'

Her words cut me like a knife. So nasty! So rude! I couldn't let her get away with this. I spun around at her and shouted:

'Just who do you think you are, Diane? What gives you the right to judge everybody else like this? You shouldn't judge me. Who are you to judge me, or my mum? You didn't even know her!'

'I know enough. Stupid cow! If she hadn't been such a bloody slag, we wouldn't be in this...'

'STOP RIGHT THERE, YOU BITCH!' I screamed at the top of my lungs. 'DON'T SAY ANOTHER WORD. NOT ONE MORE WORD. I'VE HAD ENOUGH OF YOU. YOU ARE NOT WORTHY OF MENTIONING MY MOTHER'S NAME, LET ALONE DRAGGING IT THROUGH THE MUD. SHE WAS WORTH A HUNDRED TIMES MORE THAN YOU! YOU WANT TO KNOW SOMETHING, DIANE? YOU'RE BEING JUDGED! YOU ARE BEING JUDGED!'

I was so angry, I wanted to hit her – after all the suffering she had caused me and now she had the audacity to speak of my poor dead mum like that! Fuming with rage, I stood there for a second longer, but somewhere deep inside I knew hitting her wouldn't help the situation. *No, don't let her win!* I told myself and mustering all my self-control, I managed to turn and walk away. As soon as I was out of her sight I ran, desperate to get as far away from her as possible. At the end of the road, I turned the corner and broke down completely. But the crying didn't last long – I was too angry to cry.

I can't go to school like this! I'm too wound up. In my head I was still in shock, I couldn't believe what had just happened. I never shouted in the street like that! But this time Diane had gone too far. What gave her the right to talk about my mum like that? Oh, my blood was boiling! *What to do? What to do?* I looked around me. My cousin Greg lived nearby. Now twenty-three, Greg had become a firm friend. I frequently babysat for his girlfriend Jackie and I knew that he had always got on really well with my mum, who had babysat him when he was a little boy. At least there I knew I would find some measure of comfort.

'Amanda?'

Greg was clearly shocked when he opened the door to find me on his doorstep, especially since it was still so early in the morning. For a moment I just stood there, hardly having the courage to look up. Finally, I said in a small voice: 'Can I come in please, Greg? I've had a bit of a fight with Diane. I'm really upset,' and before I'd even stepped inside the front door, I was sobbing.

'Here, come on, you!' he said in a gentle tone, taking my arm and leading me inside. 'Come here. What's up with you, eh? I'm sure it's not *that* bad! Come in and tell us all about it. Jackie's here – we'll put a brew on. Come on, sit down; stop crying now, Amanda. What's happened?'

I started to tell Greg and Jackie about the events of that morning but when I got to the part about Diane calling my mum a slag, I welled up again.

'She didn't even know her, Greg!' I wailed. 'How could she say something like that? It's cruel; it's vicious!'

By now, Greg, agitated, was pacing up and down, chain-smoking.

'Not to mention completely untrue!' he spat. 'That bloody bitch, how dare she! How DARE she! I can't believe what I'm hearing, I really can't.'

Now he stopped pacing and knelt beside me.

'Don't listen to a word that woman says, right? Your mum was such a good person, such a good, decent human being. I've always thought that. Always.'

Greg was then back to pacing and it was like he was possessed. He kept muttering to himself about how it 'wasn't right' and shaking his head.

I went on: 'Well, anyway, I didn't want to go straight to school and I couldn't tell Nan this. I didn't know who to turn to…'

'No, Amanda, you were right to come here,' Jackie said, putting her hand on my knee. 'We know you've been having a tough time with Diane.'

Suddenly Greg stopped pacing and he stood in the living room with his hands on his hips, resolute.

'Yeah, we know about the other stuff and frankly, Amanda, I've had enough of this. You're not staying there anymore – you need protection from this woman. I mean, what the fucking hell is your dad playing at? He should be sticking up for you! This shouldn't be happening. So that's it – you're not going back!'

'What? Where am I going to go?' I was shocked.

'We'll sort something out,' Greg replied. 'Don't worry about that.'

I took a deep breath and looked at Greg. He seemed strong and something in his strength felt like it passed to me. He was only a young guy but he was taking control of the situation, and for the first time, it felt like somebody was finally in my corner. *So, is this it?* I thought. *Is this the moment everything changes?* I knew this was a very big decision for me, a life-changing decision. It felt like I was standing on the edge of a cliff and I had a choice. Either run back or jump...

I thought for a minute. I thought about the months and months of misery I'd endured and the struggle I'd had to keep myself together, mentally and physically. No, there was no going back. I had no choice: I jumped.

'Okay,' I agreed. 'Okay, but I'll need some of my stuff. I've only got my schoolbag here. I've got the sneaky key Dad gave me and Diane's out now, so we could go back now, if you come with me.'

'Yeah, fine,' Greg agreed. 'We'll go back, pick up some bits and then we'll get you somewhere to stay. Don't worry, Amanda. We'll get this sorted.'

It felt good to hear him say that. Greg's anger, the way he had reacted so violently to what Diane had said about my mum, mirrored the way I was feeling inside. She had no right to go dragging up the past like that and throwing it in my face when I'd done nothing to deserve it. Greg knew what I had gone through, what we had *all* gone through as a family. It had been a terribly painful time for us all. His own grandad had died of a broken heart. For her to bring this up when she didn't even know my mother, well, it was beyond the pale.

Greg walked me back to my house, where I packed a couple of carrier bags full of clothes and toiletries. I wasn't worried about bumping into Diane – I knew she was out at one of her cleaning jobs and she wasn't aware of the spare key Dad had given me. Greg stalked the house, still spitting blood.

'Where is she now?' he asked as I flew around my room, stuffing socks and T-shirts into my bag.

'I don't know,' I said. 'One of her cleaning jobs, probably. She never tells me and frankly, I don't really care.'

As soon as we left, Greg outlined his plan.

'Look, you'll have to go to Floss's tonight, just to give me a couple of days to sort something out for you. Is that alright?'

I nodded.

So an hour later we were sat in my Nan Floss's front room, explaining the whole sorry affair.

'So you see, she can't go back there,' Greg said slowly. 'Not after what Diane said about Susan.'

'My goodness me, no!' Floss said, clutching her chest in shock. 'Did she really say those things, Amanda? I can't believe it!'

'She really did, Nan,' I said sadly.

Nan shook her head and tutted.

'Well, no, you can't stay there then. Of course you can stay here, love – you know you're always welcome.'

'Thanks, Nan,' I smiled.

'Yeah, thanks, Nan,' Greg repeated and gave me a reassuring squeeze of the shoulder. 'Chin up, girl!' he winked. 'You're going to be alright. Now I'll go round Wigram Way later and I'll talk to your dad. I'll explain everything, that you've left and you're not coming back. I suppose if he wanted to call you here, he could?'

At this I shrugged – I didn't really care one way or another anymore. I had bigger things to worry about now.

Once Greg had gone, I sat on my bed in my room in Floss's house, looking at all the little knick-knacks that I'd collected over the years. My little embroidered jewellery box, my porcelain clown figures, framed photos and my silk teddies. Memories of a childhood I was about to leave behind forever... *How had it come to this?* One thing I knew for certain, I couldn't stay here full-time – it was always so cold in Floss's house because she only ever had one radiator on to save on her heating bills. But also, Nan was a worrier. Understandable, really, after everything she had gone through, but it felt stifling at times and I knew I had to find a place of my own, where I could live my own life. It hit me then – I would probably have to give up my studies. There was only one way I could afford to live independently and that was if I had a full-time job.

That night, Nan Floss made a delicious cottage pie and I tucked in, suddenly starving hungry, then we both crashed out in front of the TV, grateful for some light relief after the tumultuous events of the day. It was only 8pm when my dad rang but already I was exhausted and ready for bed.

'Amanda?'

'Yeah. Hi, Dad,' I replied dully. I felt wrung out by all the emotional upset and the decision to finally leave home. At this moment all I really wanted was to go to sleep and forget about it all.

'Why don't you come back home, Amanda?' he sounded upset. 'Please? Please, don't leave me.'

This struck me as odd. Don't leave *him*? Who was the child here? Was I there to look after him?

I didn't respond, so he went on: 'Don't leave me with her, Amanda. She gives me bellyache! Come on home, 'Manda. I need you, I really do.'

He was pleading now and it made me angry and disgusted with him.

'No, Dad. I'm not coming back there. I can't take anymore. I can't come home like that – she made my life unbearable. Did you hear what she called me today? And my mum? Did Greg tell you the names she called us?'

'Yeah, yeah, I heard,' Dad said quickly. Dismissively, I thought. 'Look, don't listen to her or what names she calls you. I'll make it all better, I promise.'

'It's not just the names, Dad, and you know it. I don't eat there. I can't wash my clothes, or come and go when I like. You have to give me a sneaky key. I can't live like that!'

'It'll change, I promise!'

But I couldn't believe my dad's promises anymore. Look at his track record!

'No, Dad. It's too late for all that. You could have said something before now. You could have done something a month ago, six months ago even, but now it's too late. This situation has been going on a long time. She wants me out and now she's got her way! I don't think there's anything more for either of us to say. I'll be in touch. Look after yourself, okay?'

And with that, I put the phone down.

For a moment, I felt horrible, horrible about the whole situation. Everything was so up in the air. What was going to happen now? Where would I end up? I was relieved to be out of that house but at the same time my life was now so uncertain. *How am I going to earn enough money to support myself? Where am I going to live?* I stood in the corridor and felt my shoulders shake. It was all too much.

Softly, I heard my nan walk up behind me and put her arms around my shoulder.

'It'll all work out, Amanda. I'm sure of it. Come on, don't get upset – I'll make you a nice cup of tea.'

I put myself to bed early. Now, as I lay on my back, studying the cracks in the ceiling, I wondered why things were such a struggle for me. Maybe this was the way my life was destined to be. Stop. Start. Stop. Start. It didn't seem to flow easily, the way other people's lives flowed. I ran my hands along my Pierrot clown bedspread. The sad clown shed one solitary, black tear down his cheek and I put my hand over the tear – I didn't feel like crying anymore. There was too much to think about, too much to do. I looked over the framed family photos on my tallboy. There was one in a silver frame of me as a little girl, looking so happy and full of joy. It always made me smile, just looking at it. There was another of me on my mum's shoulders and also one of Dad with Terry when he was much younger. One thing was for certain – I was done with that house. Whatever happened from here, I just had to rely on myself.

I was never going back.

In my head I heard a little strumming and then the opening bars to the Bowie song I knew so well. I started to hum softly to myself and then the familiar words popped into my head: '*It's a God-awful small affair to the girl with the mousy hair*'.

I smiled briefly, then fell asleep.

CHAPTER 18

FREEDOM

I peddled hard on the uphill and then let my feet rest on the bars as I freewheeled down the other side. Ahhhh! The wind whipped my hair back and for a brief second, I closed my eyes and imagined I was flying. This was freedom!

It was 8.30am on a Thursday morning and I was on my way to my new full-time job at Knebworth House and Gardens. When I had told my good friend Sam about leaving home and needing to earn money to pay for lodgings, she said that she would go with me. It was funny – Sam didn't need to leave home; she came from a big family of five kids and was just fiercely independent. While I was full of anxiety and trepidation, she loved the idea of moving out of home. It was wonderful to have a good friend by my side. Greg found us each a room in a shared house on the outskirts of Shephall and Sam, who had worked at Knebworth the year before, managed to get us both full-time jobs for the summer.

Knebworth was a beautiful old Gothic Manor House in enormous grounds with deer. It was just a twenty-minute bike ride away, so every morning Sam and I cycled to work together. Sam was slim with brown shoulder-length permed hair and hazel-green eyes. She worked in one of the ice-cream kiosks and it was my job to look after the gift shop. It was an easy, undemanding job and usually there weren't that many visitors so I spent a good deal of time rearranging the little jam pot displays or folding tea towels. I looked forward to lunchtime when I'd meet Sam in the restaurant, and the nice Scottish lady who worked there always gave us a hot meal for free. My favourite was her delicious beef stroganoff. At the end of each day, I would cycle down the steep hill from the top of the park to where Sam was at the kiosk and we would cycle home again.

At the start, our shared house was a bit like a party house – all our friends would come to hang out because it was so much more relaxed than at their own homes. Away from parents, everyone could chill out. At first I thought I might be able to manage my schoolwork too, but after two weeks it was clear I couldn't do the job and my A-levels, so I told the head of year that I had to give up school in order to support myself. He was disappointed, but he understood. I hated having to do that, but I didn't have any choice and I vowed one day I would return to my studies.

One day, I would prove Diane wrong.

Our shared house was fun but it felt impersonal, a bit like a hostel. Everyone had their own room and we shared a kitchen, but that was it. There was no cosy lounge or living room, no communal space, and I longed for the comforts of a proper home and a decent home-cooked meal at night.

'I've got a place for you!' Greg said excitedly after he called round one day after work in the first week of June 1992.

'I've spoken to Norma, Jackie's mum, and she's happy to have you lodge with her. You'll have your own room and she'll make you a meal every night. How does £35 a week sound?'

'Yeah, that sounds good,' I said, grinning. It felt so good to have Greg looking out for me, helping me to get on my feet. I marvelled then at how lucky I was to have a lovely cousin like him and also great friends like Sam helping me, standing by my side and making this transition so much easier. Going to live with Norma sounded like a great prospect – it meant I would see a lot of Jackie, Greg and Jackie's daughter Zoe, and also that I would be somewhere homely.

From the word go, I liked Norma very much. A warm woman in her early fifties, she had short auburn hair framing a round face and deep blue eyes. She wore modern clothes, a cheery smile and she made me feel welcome in her home from the very start. Her two grown-up girls had left home, so it was just her twelve-year-old son Tom and me in the house with her. I was given the small back room in her three-bedroom terraced house in Bedwell. It was comfy, pretty, and smelled of freshly painted walls. But best of all, I was part of a family again. Most evenings, the three of us enjoyed a meal together before we relaxed in front of the TV in the living room. It was a great relief to be in a homely atmosphere, surrounded by people who liked me and wanted me there. For the first time in ages, I felt I could truly relax.

By August I had settled in well with Norma, and Sam too had managed to find lodgings in a house in the same street so we were still hanging out together every day. Now I was earning enough to pay my way and life wasn't too bad. I chose not to dwell on the situation with my family – if I found myself thinking about it and getting angry or upset, I'd shake myself out of it and go for a cycle ride or a walk. There was no point in wishing things were any different; I was just going to have to make the best of things, so I might as well enjoy my life. One thing was certain: I didn't want anything to do with my dad. I still went to visit Nan Eve and Grandad Frank most weekends, which was how I managed to stay in touch with my brother Terry, but I didn't call or go round to Dad's – I felt he had made his choices over the years and now, there was nothing left to say to each other.

One sweltering day at the end of August, Sam was round at my house and we were mucking about, trying on different make-up, when we heard the glorious tinkling music of an ice-cream van turning into our road.

'Ice cream!' we both shouted in unison and I grabbed my purse and keys as we headed out the door.

'God, I'd kill for a 99!' Sam puffed as we headed up the road, her in her little shorts and me in my light summer trousers and vest top. It was boiling hot and I was looking forward to cooling down, too – with a Fab lolly.

By the time we got to the van, there was already quite a

queue of parents being harassed by their overexcited children. We took our places and waited, watching the men in the van as they worked like mad to get everyone their orders.

'There you go, my darling!' said one of the guys as he leaned forward, holding out a perfect swirly 99 with a Flake on top.

'Now don't go eating it all at once,' he grinned at the girl before turning to us. He had dark floppy hair, piercing blue eyes and lovely smooth skin.

He fixed his steely blue gaze on me. *Wow! He's handsome.*

He seemed young too, around our age or maybe a little older.

'Alright, girls!' he said, rubbing his hands together enthusiastically. 'What's it to be?' Then he leaned forward, right out of the van, as if to get a better look. 'Blimey, you look about as hot as I feel!'

Cheeky bugger! He was flirting with me.

'Yeah, you got a pair of sizzlers there, Glen!' said the other guy in the van. He was a little older than the one serving but just as cheeky and not-bad looking either. I knew which one I liked.

'I'll have a Fab, please, *Glen*!' I said, smiling sweetly at him.

'A 99 for me!' Sam piped up.

'So, you girls local?' Glen asked as he turned the cone expertly under the nozzle of the ice-cream machine.

'I've just moved in down the road. Same as Sam – we've both got lodgings here.'

'That's funny – I live on this street too. I sort of recognise you. You didn't go to Heathcote, did you?'

'Yeah, I did, actually!'

'Thought so. I was a year above you. Well, well, well... It's nice to see a friendly face around here. If you fancy dropping by some time, I'm just over the road,' he said and pointed to a house with a red front door. 'That's me – number 28. I'm Glen, by the way, but I guess you know that already! Don't tell me... Is it Anna?'

'Amanda, actually,' I grinned.

I didn't remember seeing him in Heathcote, but then it was a very big school and it was rare to know all the kids in your own year. Glen seemed very warm and friendly and I liked him straight away.

Sam meanwhile had been joking and chatting to the other guy in the van, whose name was Sean. Eventually, after we'd paid for our ice creams, I knew what I had to do. Sam had this irritating habit of always taking first dibs on the best-looking guy in any group, which meant if I fancied someone that she liked, I didn't stand a chance. So as soon as we were out of earshot of the van, I whispered to her: 'I like that one, Glen.'

'Yeah, but I like him,' Sam pouted.

'You can't like him,' I said resolutely. I wasn't going to give way this time. 'I said it first, so that's that.'

'It doesn't matter who says it first.'

'Yeah, it does!'

We bickered all the way home, like a couple of little kids, but by the evening it was all forgotten. She knew that I had said it first, so officially, Glen was mine! The next day I went round and knocked on his door.

'Amanda!' He looked even more handsome out of his white serving smock and in his normal clothes and he seemed very happy to see me. 'What a surprise! Do you want to come in for a cold drink?'

Glen and I spent a good hour chatting and getting to know each other better. At eighteen he was in college, studying for his A-levels in Maths, English, Statistics and Business Studies, and working the ice-cream van at the weekends.

Over the next few weeks, he and I became quite close. I'd drop by his house after work and he came babysitting with me when I went round to Uncle Kevin's. At the weekends, we'd go to the park together and in the evenings we met up in a café or went to the cinema. I liked being with Glen. He was straightforward – there was no side to him, no second-guessing. You knew that when he said something, he meant it, and I found that made me feel comfortable and easy. We kissed and cuddled a few times and it was very nice but I could tell that Glen wanted us to be a proper couple and something inside me said this wasn't right. While my future was still so uncertain, I needed to feel free, so after a couple of months, I told him I didn't want to get into anything serious.

Glen looked crestfallen.

'It's just that I'm too young for a serious relationship,' I told him as we walked round the Lakes. I kept thinking about what my dad had always told me: 'Don't get married too young, live your life first.' Of course he was talking about his own experiences – he had been too young when he'd married my mum and look how that turned out! I didn't want to repeat the mistakes from the past; I didn't want to rush into a relationship when I didn't feel ready. Was I ready for a big commitment with Glen? No way! I didn't even know where

I was going to work at the end of the summer, let alone what I wanted for the rest of my life. No, it was too much while everything was still up in the air.

'There's nothing wrong with you,' I went on, as Glen asked if it was something he had said or done. I was sorry to hurt his feelings in this way. 'I just don't want to be with anyone at this time – it's too much for me.'

A week later, Nan Eve told me Dad and Diane had split up. It didn't strike me that she was terribly upset – after all, she knew everything that had gone on between Diane and me.

'They're still in the same house together,' she explained. 'But they're not, erm, a couple or anything.'

I stayed silent; I wasn't surprised. It's not like they were very close or seemed like a particularly happy couple. I shrugged and murmured: 'Oh, right.'

I didn't really know how I was supposed to take the news but some part of me felt even angrier. *Why did he wait till now to split up with her? If he didn't want to be with her, he could have left her years ago and saved us all a lot of heartache.*

Oh well, it was none of my business anymore. Besides, I had other things to focus on right now – I had my own life to live.

It was 1992 and I was seventeen years old, just about to lose my seasonal job at Knebworth House. Sam and I loved the new wave of house music that was taking over the charts and though I wasn't into drinking or drugs, I was just discovering a world of going out. One day, after work, Sam came round to my house.

'Pump Up The Jam' came on the radio and we both started bouncing up and down, trying to outdo each other with our best 'Running Man' moves until we collapsed onto the bed, exhausted and giggling with the effort.

'Hey, listen,' she said suddenly, 'I've just remembered, I heard they're looking for cleaners at the business park up the road. We'll both be out of work soon, so do you fancy doing the cleaning when that stops? It's only a couple of hours a night but it'll keep the money coming in for a while and maybe we can clean houses in the daytime, too?'

'Yeah, that's fine,' I said. *Thank God someone was thinking of me!* I was grateful to Sam for keeping me in work and as soon as September was over, we went to work in the business park, where we were given some basic training and then set to work with a few hours of cleaning each night. It wasn't difficult – just emptying bins, hoovering and polishing tables. During the day, Sam and I knocked on doors and we managed to pick up a few houses in the area too, so during the winter, we had enough money to cover our bills.

Then one evening in April 1993, a year after I'd left home, Norma dropped a bombshell.

'I'm afraid the bills have skyrocketed this year,' she said sadly. 'I'm going to have to put your rent up.'

'Oh right, to what?'

'I need £55 a week and I'll need you to buy your own shampoo and conditioner from now on too.'

'Blimey,' I said, 'that's quite a jump!'

It occurred to me she might put the rent up another £5 or £10, but adding another £20 a week was a bit steep and I wasn't sure I could manage it. I'd always paid my rent on time every Friday, no matter what, even if meant going short for a week. Some weeks we only had a couple of houses to clean and I had nothing left over at all. I'd borrow some money from Greg or Sam to tide me over, then I'd have to pay them back the following week.

After speaking to a couple of friends I discovered there was a room in a shared house in Ridge Way that was much cheaper than Norma's place, so the following week, I broke the bad news and told her I couldn't pay her what she wanted.

'It's too much money, Norma,' I said. 'I'm moving out.'

I could see she was surprised. She just said: 'Oh, okay then.' And left it at that. It was clear she thought I would pay the extra money, but I had made up my mind.

Yet it was easier said than done. I had to pack up all my things into a couple of bin liners and carry them round to a five-bedroom house where I knew no one.

That first night, I was quite scared. I sat in my bare room and listened to a couple in another bedroom arguing. It was depressing. At one point I needed a wee but I was frightened to leave my room in case I bumped into someone on the way there or back. Finally, it got too much and I bolted out of my bedroom as quick as I could. As I did so, one of the bedroom doors creaked open and an old woman in heavy make-up peered out. I nearly shrieked with fear!

Sam fell about laughing when I described my first night at the house. In fact, the next day everyone introduced themselves and in the cold light of day, I realised they were all nice people. The kitchen was clean, with solid, modern units and all the equipment worked well, so it was a comfortable place to live for a while. The other residents were all friendly and it wasn't long before they started to invite me out with them. And it was on one of these nights out that I met Lloyd, my first serious boyfriend.

Lloyd's sister was friendly with some of the girls I knew and one night I got chatting to him in the pub where we all hung out. He was very handsome – a bit like Jason Priestley from the TV series *Beverly Hills 90210* – very tall and slim, with brown hair, blue eyes and honey-coloured skin. He told me he valeted cars for a living. I couldn't say no when he asked me out, and immediately we got on really well. We hadn't been dating long when he suggested I move in with him at the home he shared with his parents, Josie and Pete.

'Won't they mind?' I asked. I had met his parents a few times and though they were lovely people, they already had a full house with Lloyd, his two sisters and one boyfriend!

'Oh no, they're cool with it,' he said casually. 'I've already asked Mum and she said it would be fine.'

'Well, I don't know. How much is the rent?'

'Oh, don't worry about that. We'll work something out.'

So after just a few months I moved into Lloyd's home. Josie and Pete were very friendly, laid-back people and made me feel welcome right from the start. I also got on very well with Lloyd's sisters. They were sporty girls like me and his twin worked in a gym. She got me going along and I was instantly hooked.

'What do you want to go to a gym for?' Nan Eve asked me one weekend. 'Do you want to get muscles like a body-builder?'

It was the first proper gym in our area and initially people were baffled that I spent so much time there.

'Oh, it's not like that, Nan!' I laughed. 'I just go and do exercise like aerobics, to keep in shape.'

Each night, Lloyd's mum cooked a delicious meal and we all helped to lay the table and clear up afterwards. On Fridays, she had a night off, so we all sorted ourselves out with a takeaway, chips or we cooked for ourselves. From Josie I learned what being a real mum meant. She had a gentle, kind way about her, so there was no shouting or bossing in this house. Whenever she asked the kids to do something, she just said something like: 'Can you hang the washing up please, Lloyd?' and it would simply get done. No messing. I learned about how to be in a family unit without tension and animosity. I also learned about communication, how to run a family home so that everyone had their little jobs and it all went smoothly; I even got some ideas about decorating too. Josie had lots of little stylish tricks to make the rooms look nice, like low-level lighting and using throws and lots of mirrors to make a room look bigger.

It was while I was living with Lloyd that my Nan Eve and Grandad Frank gave me a box of my mum's belongings that had previously been held by the police.

'The police took everything at the time,' Nan Eve explained. 'Notepads, books and things... This was the stuff they gave back.'

The first thing I saw when we opened the box was my mother's simple gold wedding band – distressingly, it was still charred black from the fire, but Grandad soon got it cleaned up so that it was gleaming again and I decided to wear it on my thumb. It was her wedding ring, not mine, so I couldn't put it on my wedding finger. Still, it was lovely to have something of hers that was so precious to her.

I was amazed to find the notebooks were filled with poems written by my mum. Many were sad, but some were deeply philosophical. I spent hours poring over her words, examining each poem, and in those words I found great comfort and a way to feel close to Mum again. At night I'd read them over and over again and I'd think about the meaning as I drifted off to sleep. I didn't need to wonder about my mum anymore; I could hear what she thought and felt in her own words:

What did you do today? Anything worthwhile?
Did you make a child smile?
Did you do a favour or good turn?
Did you help the ignorant to learn?
Did you feed the birds or clear the snow?
If you have feelings, do they show?
Did you cry, laugh, sing or weep?
Or did you hide in bed and sleep?
Get out of bed and see this day
A lot of things will come your way
People, places, time and travel
Your mind unwinds and thoughts unravel.
Or stay in bed and close your head
And do the same as when you're dead.

By Susan Lowson, 1979

CHAPTER 19

JOHN DICKINSON

'What is it, Amanda?' Lloyd asked as I held the letter in my trembling fingers. 'Are you okay? You've gone very pale.'

I suddenly felt shaky and had to sit down on the sofa in the living room.

'It's from the Victim Support service,' I said in a quiet voice. 'They want to meet me. They want to talk to me about my mum's murderer. They say I can ask them things... things about him.'

'Oh – will you meet them?'

'I suppose so. I don't know what this is about, but yeah, I think if they want to talk to me, it's probably a good idea.'

I felt a chill go through me then. It had been a long time since I'd thought about John Dickinson. Of course I had told Lloyd all about my background – it felt unfair not to share the truth with him – but I hadn't seriously considered what Dickinson was doing with his life right now. This letter brought it all back. He was still alive, out there in the real world. It made me feel strange to know that he was getting up every day, same as me, getting dressed, having breakfast, going about his normal life. *Does he ever think about my mum?* I wondered. *Does he ever feel bad about taking all that away from her? Taking her away from me?*

We arranged the meeting at my Aunty Carol's house with Carol, Nan Floss and my cousin Claire. I knew I would feel better for having my family with me but still, I was nervous when the Victim Development Managers arrived. Two women in black suits wearing very sombre expressions introduced themselves as Abigail and Beatrice and we showed them through to my aunt's living room, where Carol plied them with hot mugs of tea. The first lady, Beatrice, looked like she was in her mid-forties and had reddish-brown curly hair. She was clearly the one in charge.

'Look, we want to get straight to the point here, Amanda,' she said as soon as they were both seated. 'Since you're now eighteen, you have the opportunity to find out a bit more about John Dickinson. We can give you a bit of basic information and similarly, you can tell us a little about your experiences and how we can best help you, moving forward.'

Abigail, who had wispy blonde hair held back in a loose ponytail and a round, gentle face, added: 'We're here to support you, basically.'

I took a deep breath and Nan Floss squeezed my hand reassuringly.

'Okay,' I said. 'What can you tell me? Is he still in prison? Is he going to stay there?'

Beatrice spoke again: 'John Dickinson received two life sentences from the trial judge and we would say that the time he has been incarcerated, he has not progressed well through the system...'

'Basically, he doesn't acknowledge his crimes,' Abigail interjected.

'That's right,' Beatrice nodded curtly. 'He doesn't accept that he is guilty of the offences he was found guilty of, and therefore he is unlikely to be released from prison any time soon.'

'He doesn't accept it?' I was gobsmacked. Nan tutted and shook her head. At least he wasn't going to get out of prison, but it seemed outrageous that after all this time he should be going around, pretending he was innocent.

Still lying, I thought angrily. *He's still lying after all these years.*

'Is there anything you'd like to tell us, Amanda, about what you remember or your experiences since the attack?' asked Abigail gently, her head tilted to one side. 'We work alongside the prison services and we can feed back information to them.'

This was my chance. These people had to know the truth!

'Yes!' I said resolutely. 'I'm going to tell you exactly what happened when that man, John Dickinson, killed my mum, and also something that nobody else knows – that he tried to kill me too. I want you to know that this man is definitely guilty and, whatever he says, he shouldn't get off the hook for this.'

So I told them everything. For the first time in my life I recounted all that I remembered about the attack and the fire. I told them about how he had bashed my mum's head against the wall, and about how he told me if I stopped screaming then he'd stop doing it. I told them how he had strangled me too until I blacked out and how I'd woken up next to my dead mum on a bed that was on fire. I told them how I'd been haunted all these years by nightmares and flashbacks as a result of the trauma and what it meant to live without a mum. Finally, I showed them the scars on my legs, the physical reminder of the attack that robbed me of a normal life.

It felt good to tell my side of the story – to have these people listen to what I'd gone through. Carol and Claire stayed silent throughout, hands over their mouths as they realised the full horror of what I'd experienced. Nan Floss got up and left the room – she couldn't bear it. I felt a pang of guilt just then; I didn't want to upset my nan, but at the same time I needed these people to hear what John Dickinson had done to me. Abigail nodded sympathetically, while Beatrice scribbled furiously in the large yellow notepad on her knees.

'So you see,' I concluded, 'John Dickinson is a very dangerous man and there's no way he should be released back into society. I felt what he did to my mum, and me, was planned. Nothing happened like a fight or a row that got out of hand or made him turn spontaneously. We had both been asleep; it came from nowhere.

'You need to know this, you need to know what you are dealing with, because if he is in denial now, you can be sure he was fully aware of what he was doing at the time. Otherwise, why would he tell me to be quiet? If he were out of his mind at the time, he wouldn't have done that.'

There was a long silence then, filled only by the scraping of Beatrice's pen across the paper as she caught up with everything I had said. I was pleased by her diligence, satisfied that she was taking a comprehensive note of what I was saying. Carol sniffed and then wiped away the dampness at her eyes with the knuckle of her hand. Meanwhile, I sat bolt upright, hands locked between my knees, breathing hard, trying to keep my own emotions under control. I didn't want tears to confuse the message I was trying to get across; I wanted to keep it together.

As Beatrice finished off her notes she looked up at me: 'Thank you, Amanda. That is all very helpful.'

'We really appreciate that it wasn't easy for you to tell us all of that,' Abigail added, 'but we know it was important to you.'

At this I nodded – I didn't trust myself to speak.

'Now there's one more thing we can offer you,' said Beatrice. 'And that is the chance to meet John Dickinson in person. Some victims find this a cathartic experience, an opportunity to reconcile their feelings with their experiences and to heal from the trauma in a positive way. It can also be beneficial for the offender – in your case, it might even help John Dickinson to face up to the consequences of his actions and enable him to move towards rehabilitation.

'Obviously the meeting would happen in a totally safe way, in a supportive environment within the prison, and it will be open to you now or some time in the future. Is this something you'd like to consider?'

Fear gripped me, then.

'Meet him? No way!' I said, my heart now racing. Even the thought of coming face-to-face with this man was enough to make me panic. 'If I see him, he'll *see me* and that is something I really don't want. *Ever!* This man is dangerous, just like I told you. If he sees my face and he gets released one day, what's to stop him coming after me? No, if he sees me, it might even give him ideas. Thanks, but really, this is not something I'd ever consider, now or in the future.'

Beatrice went back to scribbling in her notebook and Abigail smiled at me: 'That's fine, Amanda. We understand.'

Understand? How could any of them understand?

'I still hear his voice sometimes,' I breathed. 'When I wake up in the middle of the night and I'm alone, I hear him shouting at me. I can control the nightmares better now, but they will always be there. *He* will always be there... in my head. I don't need to see him again.'

They left a few minutes later and Nan Floss gave me a big hug. She said I'd been very courageous to tell them everything and she apologised for leaving the room.

'Oh, Nan, you don't have to apologise, it was me – I upset you! I'm sorry,' I told her.

'At least he's staying in that prison,' she added angrily. 'They should throw away the key as far as I'm concerned. He doesn't deserve his freedom again, not ever!'

'I agree.'

'Shall I put the kettle on now, do you think?'

'Yeah, go on then, Nan. I think we all need it.'

John Dickinson.

I hated the name, hated the man.

He took so much from me. Before he murdered my mother I never doubted that the next day would be normal, that I could depend on my life being the same as the day before. But since the age of four my whole life had felt shifting, temporary and uncertain. I couldn't keep hold of anything and I never knew when it was all going to be taken from me again. Cut into my bones and you would find fear: constant, clawing fear. Although the flashbacks had faded, I now suffered from IBS, brought on by stress and constant anxiety. It had started in my early teens and felt like my stomach was twisting and turning itself inside out. The doctor prescribed sachets of Fybogel to alleviate the symptoms and regular exercise helped, but a really bad attack could leave me writhing on the floor, doubled over in pain for hours.

Worry was in my guts; it was as much a part of me as eating or breathing. That feeling of always looking over my shoulder, wondering and worrying what disaster might be round the corner, that was the real cause of my pain – and nothing could make that go away.

So, no, I didn't want to see John Dickinson. I didn't want to invite him back into my world.

CHAPTER 20

FINDING
MY FEET

'Alright?' my dad asked, smiling nervously from the doorstep.

It had been four years since I'd last seen him and in that time, it didn't seem he'd changed all that much. He was still slim, smartly dressed with just a hint of grey at the temples of his dark hair.

'Yeah, good, Dad – you?' I replied and he nodded.

'You look well,' he said, giving me the once-over. 'Healthy.'

'Yeah? Thanks, Dad. Well, you know, I exercise a lot and I eat well.'

'You a vegetarian?' Dad had always been convinced of the health benefits of giving up meat and I winced then as I recalled the horrible bean stews I'd been forced to eat as a child.

'I do try, Dad, but I like my fish and chicken too much. My friend and I, we call ourselves fin-wing-tarians!'

209

He laughed out loud then and, to my relief, it broke the tension.

'Ha! Fin-Wing-tarians!' he repeated jovially. 'Very good! Very clever!'

'Come on then,' Nan Eve said as she bustled through from the kitchen with a full teapot and a plate of biscuits. 'Let's all have a cuppa, shall we? Sit down. Sit down.'

I was twenty-one years old and I'd already moved on from Lloyd. We'd had a good relationship for three years, but by then I was ready to take the next step.

'Why don't we get our own place?' I had suggested to him on numerous occasions. I was now working part-time at the crèche in the gym where I trained. It was a lovely morning job and I enjoyed playing with the little ones and chatting to the other girls who worked there. I felt it was time to move on in my living arrangements too.

'Nah, we can just keep living here,' he'd replied.

I had found it frustrating. I couldn't live at his parents' house forever – I had dreams of having my own home and children one day. It was the beginning of the end for us and when he started working nights, we just drifted apart. There was no big drama when we split up. I simply found new lodgings with the woman who ran the crèche where I worked, and that was that.

By now, I was also working part-time in the housekeeping department of the Lister Hospital, taking the trolley round and giving out drinks and meals. It was a good little job and I enjoyed the interactions with the patients. They were always pleased to see me and it felt like I was doing something positive with my life. But being around very sick people day in, day out reminded me that none of us are around forever and it struck me that I hadn't spoken to my own father in years. That made me sad. One way or another, he was my dad and I loved him. Whatever anger I'd felt towards him about how I had left home had now faded.

'I think I'd like to see Dad again,' I told my Nan Eve the following weekend. I knew that they kept in touch, and it was the best way to make contact with him.

Sure enough, the following week, Nan rang Dad to tell him I was there and invited him to pop in for a cup of tea. At first, it was really weird seeing him again. There was so much I wanted to say to him and at the same time, there was a big distance between us now. It had been so long, we had to find ways to reconnect again. We chatted about general things at first. Dad collected stamps and coins, and when I was little, I took an interest too. Now we had a long chat about the latest coins he'd found for his collection.

As he left, I gave him a hug: 'It was good to see you, Dad.'

'Yeah, likewise,' he said. I knew that he was no longer with Diane, but I had heard from Nan that they lived in the same house for a long time.

'Diane still at your place?' I asked.

'No,' he said. 'She's moved out now. She found herself another man.'

Blimey, I did not expect that!

I didn't pry any further – frankly, I wasn't interested in Diane and I felt that at this early stage, it was best to leave that whole subject alone. I kissed him once on the cheek and he left. We had a long way to go before our relationship was repaired, and maybe it would never fully recover, but at least we were talking again. And we had started building a bridge between our lives. Whatever choices he'd made in the past as a father, I had to forgive and start afresh. After all, I only had one parent and for better or worse. My grandparents wouldn't be around forever.

Now that I was no longer a ward of court, I was allowed to go on foreign holidays. Apart from two dismal, grey day trips to Dunkirk with the school, I'd never been abroad. For the first time in my life I started to travel. At eighteen, my Chalkley family paid for me to go to Menorca with them all and it was incredible! I couldn't believe the heat from the sun – it was like nothing I'd ever experienced. The food too was amazing – the tomatoes were huge and plump, the seafood was fantastic and the local dishes like paella and tapas were delicious. I was hooked! After that, I made sure I went on at least one nice holiday a year with Lloyd and we travelled to the Greek Islands and even swam with the dolphins in Israel. Yes, I was really starting to expand my horizons...

'Go on...' Jess urged. 'Talk to him!'

One Tuesday afternoon in December 1996 I was on my rounds when I spotted the emergency dentist on one of the wards I visited. My friend Jess, who worked as an orderly, knew I fancied him, but I was always too shy to go up and speak to him. He was very handsome, with jet-black hair, hazel eyes and a strong Roman nose. I thought he looked very exotic, foreign maybe.

212

'Do you think he's Spanish?' I had asked Jess one day as I admired him from afar.

'Maybe,' she murmured. 'Or Italian?'

'He could be Greek!' I added, recalling the stocky, moustached men I'd met on my travels.

'Well, whatever he is, you'll never find out unless you talk to him!' Jess sighed impatiently.

So, screwing up my courage, I went over to talk to him. He had just finished examining a patient and was standing at the nurses' station, filling out a form.

I coughed, then started nervously: 'So... erm... I've seen you...'

At that very moment the matron boomed at him: 'We've got two more patients for you to see this afternoon. Do you think you can fit them in?'

'Erm,' the handsome dentist said, looking at his watch, 'well, we'll have to be quick. Come on, then!'

And he marched off. I was left standing there, my pathetic attempt at conversation left hanging in the air. My cheeks flared red as I shuffled from side to side, trying to look like I was standing there for a reason. Sheesh! I felt like a total numpty. *What terrible timing!*

There were few more near misses like that until finally, determined not to be beaten, I marched straight up to the busy dentist in the middle of his rounds and shoved my hand towards him.

'I'm Amanda,' I said boldly. 'I've seen you here a lot but I haven't had the chance to introduce myself.'

'Mehdi.' He took my hand in his and immediately I felt a

bolt of attraction shoot through me. 'I've seen you around too. Lovely to meet you, Amanda.'

It turned out Mehdi had been keen to say hi to me too but he was a bit shy. He was from Iran, which was fascinating to me as I knew very little about the country. It wasn't long before he asked me out for a drink.

'I've just come out of a relationship,' I warned him. 'Drinks are fine but just so you know, I don't want to rush into anything.'

'That's fine by me,' said Mehdi.

Mehdi worked in Stevenage and had digs in the Lister Hospital, but he lived mainly in his mother's flat in Ealing, West London. After the Islamic Revolution in 1979, his family had fled Iran because they didn't support the religious state. His father had worked his way up through the army ranks and his mother was a teacher. Mehdi had been educated privately and despite our vastly differing backgrounds, we shared a common outlook. He was a fun, ambitious guy and it wasn't long before he got me down to London to stay with him in his flat. Since he was also keen on keeping fit, he took me to Earls Court Gym and introduced me to a whole new world of nightclubs in London. Before Mehdi came along, I'd always been a bit wary of going to The Big Smoke. I was fearful by nature and London seemed so big and impersonal.

'Don't worry about anything,' Mehdi reassured me. 'You're okay – you're with me.'

So I met some of his friends and the first club he took me to was the Emporium in Soho. I loved it! It was so vibrant and exciting and I could spend all night dancing. Occasionally I had a few drinks but I didn't go mad and drugs were definitely not for me – no, it was the music and the atmosphere I loved.

After that there was no stopping me. I was up in London every weekend, trying out all the clubs. One Saturday it was Tramp, then it was Chinawhite, Café de Paris and the Atlantic Bar & Grill. By the time I was twenty-three, I was an experienced and dedicated clubber, taking the train into London every Friday and heading back to Hertfordshire for my job on Monday morning.

'Why don't you learn to drive?' Mehdi suggested.

'I've tried that,' I said. 'I did lessons at eighteen and then I took my test but I got so nervous during the manoeuvres, I flunked it.'

In fact, I had been thinking about going back for lessons again for some time, but now that I was going up to London so much, it made sense.

'Just do a few more lessons and then I'll take you out,' suggested Mehdi. 'You can get some practice in my car. It's all about experience with driving and the more you're out on the road, the more confident you'll become.'

Mehdi was as good as his word and he let me drive his car until I was up to taking the test again. I passed third time around. It went like a dream! All my manoeuvres were perfect and I even managed a very competent 'reverse around the corner'. I felt calm, confident and secure, like a Formula One driver! To celebrate, I went out and bought my first car: a Citroën. I felt very grown-up all of a sudden, driving around Stevenage in my very own car.

Meanwhile, on the advice of the owner of the crèche where

I worked, I took an Open University Bookkeeping course from home. I wanted to better myself and it was something I had been thinking about for some time. Even so, I was surprised when I aced my exams. Now a qualified bookkeeper, I gave up my job in the Lister Hospital and started working for my Uncle Kevin's company and for a little shop in Knebworth too. Later that same year, I spotted an advert in the local paper for the deputy manager of an after-school club. I loved the idea of managing fun activities for kids, and the genius part of this plan was that it was based in a school, which meant it was a safe environment. For the first time in my life, I went after a job that I really wanted and I got the position! I was thrilled. This was what I wanted to do with my life – work with children doing fun, creative activities in an environment that allowed them to express themselves.

The set-up worked well. At the end of each school day, myself and the other club staff picked up the children from their schools and brought them back to our club. They'd have a drink and a biscuit and from there, it was up to them from 3pm till 6pm. They could play on the outside equipment, do some painting or craft activities, or just read or chat to their friends. In the winter we made biscuits, Christmas decorations and stockings, and in the summer we played a lot of sports like rounders, cricket and football. It was a great job and the energy and enthusiasm from the kids was infectious. I loved the fact that here, at the club, they could be themselves, with no one telling them what to do, and I also knew if an after-school club had existed when I was growing up, I would have loved it – it was a great way to give children some free time.

So all in all, life was pretty good – I worked for my uncle in the mornings and did the kids club each afternoon. Mehdi and I decided to take the next step and we moved into a little cottage in a village just outside Stevenage. Sadly, we found out pretty soon after moving in together that it wasn't to be. I suppose in the back of my mind, I knew we weren't compatible. He was a lovely man but we were both feisty characters. He had such a strong personality and he never let things go. If we argued, he would carry it on and on until I got so fed up with him, I just wanted to leave. In the end, I did. Four years after we first got together, I ended the relationship and moved out of our cottage into a flatshare. Now I was twenty-five – the same age my mum had been when she lost her life.

I thought about this a lot. I thought about the kind of person I had become and the way I had lived my life until now. I'd been independent for the last seven years, and in that time I had spread my wings, going into London at the weekends, holidaying in far-flung destinations, trying out different jobs, getting new qualifications, learning to drive and dating different men. I thought about my mum and how she had become trapped so early on in her life, how her opportunities and experiences had very quickly become limited. She didn't drive, she relied on public transport, and she had become responsible for a child when she was just twenty-one. I can see how that might have contributed to her depression. I knew I looked like Mum, but in many ways our life experiences had been very different. There had been a time when I was convinced I would die young, just like her, that I wouldn't live past twenty-five, but gradually I had shed these fears. I had grown up since that time; I'd found my feet.

Her poems still meant a great deal to me and I read them often, memorising many of them off by heart. In my purse, I kept a hand-written version of her poem 'Suffer we must ever do, if to ourselves we are true'. I felt it was a good, honest message and one that gave me courage when I wasn't feeling strong. Carving my path in life would always be easier if I was true to my feelings. Other poems made me reflect on how I coped with the world around me, and I hope, helped to make me a better person. She may not have been by my side but I felt my mother taught me well in my adult life.

Do you hear the silence?
Have you seen the violence?
Do you shout for noise?
Do you mend broken toys?
Do you cry for the lonely?
Do you long for somewhere homely?
Do you feed the hungry child?
Do you tame the dog that's wild?
Do you put down your sword?
Do you pray to our Lord?

By Susan Lowson

One day in February 2000, just as I was leaving my Uncle Kevin's office, I noticed a man leaving the block of offices opposite. For a moment, I just stood there, staring. He looked

218

oddly familiar, this tall, broad man... And then suddenly it struck me: Glen! It was my ex-boyfriend Glen – a little older, broader and more manly, but it was definitely him.

'Glen!' I called out and he turned round. As he did so, his eyes widened in delight: 'Amanda!'

We got chatting and it turned out Glen ran his own courier company from this office and also owned a balloon shop a little further down, run by his mum and sister. I admired his drive and ambition – he had clearly been busy in the years since we'd split up. He looked different too; he had filled out and now had a very manly physique. *And was it my imagination, or was he more handsome too?* I wondered. The attraction that had been there all those years ago was definitely still there. Suddenly, I remembered my job at the kids club.

'I've got to go!' I said, looking at my watch. 'I work at an after-school club for children.'

'What are you doing this evening?' Glen asked. 'I'd love to take you out for a drink and a catch-up.'

'Yeah, that'd be lovely,' I agreed.

Glen had such a warm, gentle way about him. I was thrilled to meet up with him again. How strange that he happened to work opposite my uncle! Was this fate?

That night we met up in the Three Horseshoes, a village pub just outside Stevenage, and caught up over dinner on what we'd both been up to over the past nine years. The conversation flowed easily between us and by the time we were on our main courses, Glen was in a confessional mood.

'You know, I always had strong feelings for you, Amanda,'

he said shyly. 'I was really upset when you finished with me. I think I knew really early on that I wanted to be with you.'

'Really?' I was surprised and secretly, very pleased. 'I was only seventeen, Glen. I didn't know what I wanted then.'

'And how do you feel now?' he asked, suddenly locking me with an intense gaze. My tummy flipped upside down.

'I don't know,' I blushed, looking down at my plate. 'I suppose we'll have to see. Are you asking me out again?'

'Yeah,' he laughed. 'Is that alright?'

'Yeah,' I grinned back, and he took my hand in his.

The second time around with Glen was different. We had always got on very well, but now, my feelings for him were much stronger and I felt more attracted to him. Maybe I had changed. I wasn't looking for the same things I had wanted as a teenager – I didn't want a man to show me a good time or exciting nights on the tiles. I valued kindness, warmth, manners and understanding. I wanted someone I could share my life with.

One day I invited him to come out for a run with me. Seeing as I had always kept very fit, I was worried he wouldn't be able to keep up.

'Don't worry if you fall behind,' I reassured him. 'We can just agree to meet up at the park gates afterwards if we split up.'

'Park gates? Yeah, okay,' he agreed, looking very serious, and then we took off.

I should have known better! From the start, Glen was way out in front of me, putting me through my paces, tiring me out and even jogging on the spot while I struggled to catch up.

'Jesus, Glen!' I panted as I finally reached him. 'You're really fit!'

'Yeah, I run marathons,' he grinned wickedly.

'You bastard! Why did you let me think you were a beginner?'

'Because it was really, really funny,' he said, and with that fell about laughing. Red-faced, I started laughing, too. I felt like a right muppet!

That winter we went on holiday to Cyprus. It was wonderful being in a hot country while Stevenage was blanketed by grey, drizzly skies. We hung out on the beach, swam in the sea and ate out every night in lovely tavernas. It was pleasing that Glen was now a vegetarian too, just like my dad, and between us, we hoovered up mountains of hummus, pitta bread and tzatziki. My Uncle Kevin, his partner Sarah and their kids were also on holiday with us, so it was fun to spend time with them too.

On New Year's Eve we were rushing to get ready – we had arranged to meet Sarah and Kevin in the bar of the hotel before the big party started at 8pm. I had slipped into the fitted silver dress I'd brought along for the occasion. It was gorgeous, with a swirly black velvet pattern on the back. I had just finished putting on my ruby-red lipstick in the mirror at the dressing table in the hotel room when I turned to look at Glen. He was very smart in a blue shirt that really brought out his piercing blue eyes.

I started to walk towards the door.

'Just, erm, wait a minute, Amanda,' he said, suddenly looking at me anxiously.

'What is it?' I whipped around and there he was, on his knees, holding open a tiny box, whose contents glimmered and sparkled in the overhead light.

'Amanda Lowson, will you marry me?'

CHAPTER 21

TWO WEDDINGS

'Are you ready?' Dad asked as he took my arm.

We stood together outside pretty St Nicholas' Church in Stevenage on 25 August 2001. I watched as a little white cabbage butterfly fluttered through the church grounds, passing the rhododendron bushes and the ash trees as it dipped and floated along the path, finally coming to rest on an ancient gravestone. There, it parted its wings once before pulling them closed again, as though breathing a sigh of relief. I patted the moisture that had formed on my top lip, being careful not to smudge my lipstick. It was midday and the sun beat down mercilessly. My hand sweated as I held my pink-and-white bouquet tightly in my left hand while my right adjusted the cape at my neck. *Yes*, I nodded at my dad.

I was ready to get married.

When Glen had proposed in Cyprus, I had accepted straight

away. There was no doubt in my mind that we were right together and I was overwhelmed by the ring he had chosen: a beautiful row of seven diamonds set in a traditional gold band. I had never been given anything so valuable in my life and when we went on a short cruise to Egypt in the New Year, it felt amazing to stand on the Great Pyramids of Giza wearing my stunning engagement ring. The New Year, the ring, the start of my new life... I truly felt as if I was on top of the world!

From the word go, I knew I wanted a church wedding, and now that Dad and I were getting along well again, I wanted him to give me away. But that was about as far as it went when it came to traditional wedding conventions. The main thing was that everyone we invited would feel happy and comfortable, so I ignored all the old rules about seating, like mixing up the bride and groom's family. I had invited three people from my dad's side – Dad, Terry and Nan Eve – and around twenty-five members of the Chalkley family. I didn't invite Diane of course, and nobody questioned this.

Sadly, we had lost my Grandad Frank three years earlier from non-Hodgkin's lymphoma. It had been a difficult time – he didn't want a lot of fuss made and refused treatment. He lost a lot of weight very quickly and became frail and unable to climb the stairs so he slept downstairs, where Nan Eve tended to him. She cared for him day and night, right up until the end, because he didn't want to go to a hospice. It was very hard on her – seeing him so ill, so painfully thin – but she coped extremely well and when he finally slipped away, I think it was a relief that his suffering was finally at an end. Since then

Nan had been on her own and though I had worried for her at first, making sure to visit every week, after a few months it was clear she was stronger than I imagined, taking comfort in her old routine and way of doing things.

'Don't you want to mix the tables up?' Carol had asked when I told them about my plans to keep all the families together in their own groups at the wedding breakfast. My aunt was a stickler for tradition and even my cousin Claire put in her two pennyworth that as my chief bridesmaid she thought she ought to be sat next to the best man. But I wasn't budging. The two sides of my own family hadn't spoken to each other in over twenty years and I wasn't going to try and force anyone into an awkward meeting. No, I wanted everyone to be as comfortable as possible, which meant keeping families together.

'No, Glen and I are quite happy with things as they are, thanks,' I replied coolly. 'We've discussed this and it's what we want. We don't really care about tradition. Nowadays everyone just does what's right for them, right?'

'I suppose,' said Carol, though she clearly didn't agree with me.

'Look, it's not like I come from a traditional family set-up, is it?' I pointed out. 'Why would anyone expect me to stick to all the old conventions?'

It was 2001 and women like me had earned the right to say how we wanted to get married. Certainly, I was paying for a good proportion of my own wedding and Glen was picking up the rest of the bill, so it was up to us what we did. To me the one thing that mattered most was making sure my mum was involved. If there was one person I wanted more than anyone else, it was her and yet she couldn't be with me on my special day, but I would make damn sure she was involved every step of the way.

'Nan, what date did they get married?' I called out to my Nan Floss one Saturday when I was round at hers, poring over Mum's old wedding album. I'd seen these pictures many times over the years but still, I never tired of looking at them. Now, I was making a special effort to find little details that I could pick out and use at my own wedding. I liked the colours of my mum's bouquet – blush pink and white – maybe I'd have the same? Here was the main picture of the whole wedding party – I named them all in my head as I scanned the photo from left to right. There was Bill, Floss's brother, at the end in the blue tie, then there was Dad's pal Geoff, Grandad Frank, Nan Eve, Uncle Kevin, my dad, mum in her simple but elegant wedding gown, my cousin Greg as a little boy in front of Nan Floss, Geoff's wife Marion in platforms, Aunty Carol, Uncle Mick holding my cousin Claire, who was just a babe in arms, and right at the end, my Grandpa Bill. It wasn't a big wedding party by any stretch – we had invited over sixty guests to our wedding, which felt huge.

Now I studied the background, the sparse, empty branches and brown leaves. It must have been autumn.

'It was 2 November,' Nan shouted back from the kitchen, 'a Saturday. Cold, cold day it was.'

I noticed Nan Eve wrapped up in her dark fur and matching hat. Suddenly, something occurred to me: late autumn 1974? I was born the following April – 1975 – which meant my mum was already pregnant with me. It was a shotgun wedding! My heart started to race. Now I knew why she had rushed into marriage.

'I suppose I was in this picture too then!' I joked when Nan came in, carrying a steaming pot of tea.

'Yes, I suppose you were,' she said a little sadly.

I didn't say anything. Nan placed the pot carefully down on the doily in the middle of the table and fussed about, adjusting the brown knitted cover and smoothing down the creases on the tablecloth. Then she sat down.

'What?' she asked, as I looked at her.

'Oh, I don't know!' I threw my hands up in the air, exasperated. 'Isn't there something you want to tell me about this? About Mum being pregnant when she got married?'

'Nothing much to say, Amanda,' she replied, picking up the lid of the pot and stirring the contents.

I didn't say anything more, just waited for her to explain.

'Look, that's the way you did things back then,' she went on. 'Oh, I know it's all different now and women can have their babies out of wedlock, but in those days it wasn't *done*. Your mother wanted to do things right. Nobody *made* them get married. Your mum, well, she had high hopes. She loved your father very much and she really wanted it all to work out.'

'And when it didn't, I suppose that made her quite depressed,' I added, biting my nails.

'Yes, it did,' Floss sighed.

Still, there was a tiny niggling thought in the back of my mind.

'I hate to think I was the reason…' I started.

'Now, don't you say that,' Nan scolded. 'Don't even think that! Your mother, well, she was very strong-willed when she wanted to be. She wanted to live her own life, she wanted to be independent, and more than anything, she wanted a baby from your father because she loved him to distraction. When you came along, she was beside herself with happiness.

'She adored you. *Adored* you! Wouldn't let you out of her sight, wouldn't even leave the house, and that's when she started to get ill, when she started to get things all out of proportion. Of course, that made things hard for the two of them – her not going out at all. She didn't even want him to leave the house to go to work. Well, it was an illness, wasn't it? She went to the doctor's to get pills for it, but by then your dad, he'd had enough.'

She paused and turned the wedding album round to face her. Her fingers brushed over Mum's face and her eyes filled with tears.

'I don't know why she found life so very hard,' she said, her voice quivering with emotion. 'Perhaps... perhaps it was always in her... this... this... intensity. This *feeling* things too much. But you can be sure of one thing, you were the apple of her eye.'

Now, as I heard the organ strike up the 'Wedding March', I let my dad take my left arm and slowly, we began to walk forward, our strides exactly in time with one another. I held my cascading bouquet of roses, lilies and baby's breath in front of me, while the pink-and-white heart-shaped floral display, which spelt out 'Mum', hung from my wrist. As we moved up the aisle towards the font, I caught the eyes of well-wishing friends and family. I felt their love then, all their genuine happiness and good feeling like a tide of emotion rolling towards me. And as we passed each pew, I thought I sensed another presence by my side, like the gentle touch of a hand on my right shoulder.

Mum. My mum is here today!

'You're beautiful!' Glen mouthed as I took my place beside him in the church and I smiled appreciatively. I was pleased with my simple white silk BHS dress with the princess-style gown round my shoulders, topped off with a tiara and tiny silver cross earrings. The ceremony seemed to go by in a blur – Glen was handsome in his grey suite, white shirt and gold cravat, and he never once stumbled as he repeated his vows. Beside him, also dressed in a gold cravat, was Sean, his best man, whom I had first met at the ice-cream van all those years before. It felt so right, making our commitment to each other in front of all our family and friends, with my Aunty Carol as our official witness. The reception was all booked and ready in a hotel down the road, but there was one very important thing I needed to do before the celebrations began.

'Just here is fine,' I told the limo driver as he stopped outside Almond Lane Cemetery. Glen and I got out together, hand in hand, and we walked towards my mother's grave. As we approached, Glen gave my fingers a reassuring squeeze then let go of my hand and nodded. He stayed where he was as I walked on to the graveside, alone in my white bridal gown.

'Mum?' I said quietly as I approached her headstone. There was still the framed photo of her on the grave, though now the picture was faded from the sun. I knelt down next to it and placed the floral tribute on it, the one that spelt 'MUM'.

'Mum, did you see me today? I married Glen. I'm very happy, Mum, and we're very much in love.'

I wanted to say more but I couldn't speak. I knew she had been there with me in the church, next to me; I had felt her nearby. It was funny how, after all these years, I could still feel her love for me so strongly. *Not a day goes by when I don't think of you, Mum*, I told her now in my head, the way I had always done. *I love you and I wish you had been there in person. I miss you so much. I hope you are pleased for me, Mum. I hope I have made you proud.*

For a few minutes, I stayed there, just listening to the excited birds, trilling to each other, back and forth, watching branches sway in the breeze and taking a moment to compose myself. Just then, a small white cabbage butterfly fluttered to a rest on Mum's headstone and I smiled in recognition. Then I got up, smoothed down my dress and turned back to my new husband and my new life as a married woman.

The party was wonderful – we had a sit-down wedding breakfast at the Cromwell Hotel with Buck's Fizz on arrival and in the evening a bar, buffet, more guests and a disco. The tables had been beautifully dressed with balloons and flowers in pink and white by Glen's mum and sister. And we had endless photos taken on the lawn with all our family, as well as my seven bridesmaids – a mix of family relations – and one pageboy, Glen's eight-year-old nephew Ashley. Best of all, Dad made a really lovely speech. He said Glen and I were a great couple and we were really good for each other.

At the very end, just as he was wrapping up, he said something that caught me off-guard: 'Amanda, I'm so proud of you and I know that your mum would be proud of you, too.'

It was so unexpected. I never usually heard my dad talk about my mum as he found it difficult. Including her in his speech like this, in front of everybody on my big day, meant the world to me. That one touching tribute made up for so much that had gone on between us, and after the big toast, I gave him a massive hug and whispered: 'Thank you. I love you, Dad.'

When all the toasts and speeches were over, Glen and I took to the floor for the first dance, to Louis Armstrong's 'We Have All The Time In The World', a very special song for both of us. As he took my hand and placed his other hand at my waist, I looked up into his eyes, my own shining with love.

'Happy?' he asked.

'Yes,' I whispered, placing my head on his shoulder, 'very, *very* happy.'

We moved slowly as the rich, deep voice of Louis Armstrong filled the room, assuring us we had all the time in the world for life and love.

I suppose in the back of my mind I must have felt a little worried about the two sides of my family meeting for the first time in twenty-two years, but in the end everyone was fine with each other. They recognised that this was a wedding and not a place to be hostile. All in all, it had been a wonderful day.

We had our wedding night at the hotel and I was thrilled to wake up the next day as Mrs Wright. A few days later, we flew to the elegant coastal town of Estoril in Portugal for our honeymoon. Known as the 'Portuguese Riviera', we had chosen Estoril for its quiet, old-world charm, grand 1930s hotels, gorgeous stone villas, golden beaches and perfectly manicured lawns and gardens. It was a cut above the usual beach-holiday fare. We stayed in a lovely hotel overlooking the sea and spent two glorious weeks on the beach, enjoying some peace and quiet after all the work and effort of organising our wedding. It would have been perfect, except that right at the end of the holiday, a few days before we were due to fly home, two planes ploughed into the Twin Towers in New York. From where we were sitting, it felt like the end of the world.

All the guests gathered in the lounge, glued to the television, hands covering their mouths in horror. I didn't even understand it properly at first – I was confused. Why was there a second plane? In my mind, I thought it was an emergency plane that had crashed accidentally. I couldn't work it out.

'No, this isn't an accident,' Glen said grimly as he held me by the shoulders. 'This is very serious. It's a terrorist attack.' We could hardly believe it when in turn each tower came crashing to the ground. This was unbelievable! How could all those people be dead? It was awful beyond words.

At least Glen and I were there together. I don't know how I would have coped if I was alone. In that chaotic, nervous atmosphere, nobody knew where the terrorists might strike next and it felt like everyone was on high alert for the next attack. Uncertainty again. I recognised it immediately – the sense that everything could be taken from you in a moment. Now suddenly the feeling had spread to everyone around me and I found it disturbing. Fear and anxiety were noticeable in the way people moved, the way they talked, and the way they kept to their own little groups. An eerie silence fell over the guests in the hotel. From then on, everyone spoke in hushed whispers. Nobody could relax anymore; we all just wanted to get home.

Heightened security measures were introduced straight away, which made the journey through Lisbon Airport very scary. Burly and severe-looking armed guards in bulletproof uniforms strode through the airport terminus, all carrying large, terrifying rifles in their hands. The flight back was unusually quiet and tense as we silently prayed for it to be over and I didn't fully relax until I was back in our two-bedroom home in Stevenage. The world had changed overnight and I had no idea of the far-reaching consequences of that one terrible day in September. All I knew was that Glen and I were lucky to have found each other again and now that I was a twenty-six-year-old married woman, I was ready for the next chapter in my life.

CHAPTER 21

MOTHERHOOD

God knows why they call this morning *sickness!* I thought to myself as I clung to the white porcelain bowl of the toilet at 6.30pm on 20 May 2002. In my case it was morning, noon and night sickness! After a whole day at work feeling nauseous I had come home and thrown up. My throat was sore, there was a nasty taste of bile in my mouth and my vision swam.

Oh God, here I go again...

'Are you alright in there?' Glen called out from the living room.

'*Bleurgh!*' My whole body buckled and contorted as the convulsions came over me. There was nothing left to throw up, so I was just dry retching and praying it would be over soon.

'Do you want a glass of water?' Glen shouted, his voice full of concern. I wished I could answer him but I had no breath left in me. Exhausted and wrung out, I sat back on my heels, wiped away the spit from my chin and panted.

Of course I was thrilled to be pregnant. We had started trying for a child a few months after the wedding but it hadn't happened straight away, so we were both delighted when the home pregnancy test showed up positive. Still, I had no idea I was going to feel this rotten in the first few months.

'Why don't you slow down a bit?' Glen urged when I finally managed to crawl out of the bathroom and slump onto the sofa opposite him.

'I like my work,' I breathed, closing my eyes now to rest.

'Yes, well, maybe you just need to take things a bit easier.'

He had a point – I hadn't changed my routine since finding out I was expecting. I still worked for my uncle in the mornings and then ran the Fun Club in the afternoons. Since the old manager had left, I'd been promoted, so now I had a lot more responsibility. It was busy, but that's the way I liked it.

In the end it was the baby that forced me to slow down. It was mid-December and I was seven months pregnant. By now the morning sickness had eased and I was enjoying my food again so I had arranged to take Glen out for a fancy Christmas meal at the smart eatery Brocket Hall as a special treat. Jean-Christophe Novelli was the famous and highly celebrated chef there. While it was just the two of us, I wanted us to have as much fun as possible, but the day before we were due to go, I started to get terrible cramps across my belly.

'*Owww, owww, owww!*' I winced, doubled up on the sofa. I hadn't put on too much weight during my pregnancy and my bump was all out front and very neat.

'I think we'd better phone the hospital,' said Glen.

'It's just Braxton Hicks!' I wailed. 'They'll tell me it's Braxton Hicks.'

I had learned about this condition through antenatal classes. We were told that it feels a bit like real contractions but actually it's just your muscles in spasm, getting ready for giving birth. It must be Braxton Hicks, I reasoned, because it was far too early for anything else.

'Maybe, but still, best to check,' he said decisively. The next thing I knew, Glen was driving me to the Lister Hospital, with me protesting all the way.

It was only when they had me hooked up to all the machines and worried-looking nurses came and went from my bedside that I started to feel concerned.

'Is everything alright?' I asked one of the nurses as she took my pulse. 'Is the baby okay?'

'You're having contractions,' she replied as she scanned the monitor above my head.

'Contractions?' Now I was worried. 'But it's too soon. The baby isn't due till February.'

'Yes, I know.' She looked at me sympathetically and put a reassuring hand on my shoulder. 'Look, we're doing all we can and we can give you something to try and slow down the contractions. Nobody wants this baby to come now, but just in case, we can also give you steroid injections to help the baby's lungs. Just in case. Okay?'

I felt tears well up behind my eyes as I heard this and Glen, who was by my side, took my hand and gave it a reassuring squeeze.

'It'll be okay,' he said. 'It'll be fine.'

But that first night was terrifying and for the first time I was flooded with doubts: I had assumed that the pain was Braxton Hicks but I'd been wrong. My baby wasn't even born yet and already I was screwing things up! What if I got other things wrong when I was actually a mother? For the first time I really began to worry about whether I was going to make a good mum. After all, it wasn't like I had my own mum by my side to guide and help me. *What if the baby is born premature? Will it survive? How will I cope?* Until then I had only really thought about being pregnant and dealing with the day-to-day difficulties presented by my own body. Now I started to consider that the baby was actually another life, another person who would one day be separate from me. It was scary.

Thankfully, as daylight broke in the ward, I realised the contractions had lessened – now I was only getting a vaguely tight feeling across my bump every now and then. It felt like the danger had passed.

'Can I go home soon?' I asked the matron next time she came round to put the pads on me to monitor the baby's heartbeat.

'No, you will not be going anywhere soon,' she barked fiercely. 'Not until we know for sure the contractions have stopped.'

I stayed a second night on the ward and as I lay awake in bed that night, I realised this was serious now: I had to slow down for the sake of the baby. So, as 2003 began, I took it easy. I still worked full-time but now I took regular breaks and when I could, I delegated the more physically demanding tasks to my staff at Fun Club. I became more aware of the importance of eating small, regular meals and staying hydrated. I didn't want to put my baby at risk of a premature birth if I could help it, and thankfully I went to full-term.

At 3am on the morning of 18 February 2003, I was woken by a strange gushing sensation down below. Lifting up the duvet, I saw that the bedsheet was drenched.

'Glen,' I whispered to my husband's sleeping back. 'Glen, my waters have broken.'

He quickly sprang into action and called the hospital but they told us to wait until the morning to come in. Soon, my contractions started and as the hours passed, they grew stronger and stronger. At 8am, Glen drove me to the maternity ward of the Lister Hospital but when they checked me I was only 2cm dilated, so they sent me home again. There, we waited as the contractions came harder and closer together. By midday, they were so strong and so close that I barely had time to recover from one before another wave of pain overtook me. I even had an urge to push, so Glen insisted we go back to hospital.

'Yes, you're 8cm dilated,' the midwife smiled. 'You're going to have this baby soon. What is your birth plan?'

'Diamorphine,' I told her. I had heard that diamorphine would help take the edge off the worst of the contractions and that's what I really needed now. At first the early contractions had been manageable but now they were very painful and I was getting worn out. But just minutes after taking the diamorphine, my contractions ceased: I couldn't feel anything anymore, I realised.

'What's happened?' I asked. 'Why has it all stopped?'

'This can happen,' the midwife explained. 'Not often, but it can happen.'

For a while nothing happened at all – the midwives monitored me as we waited for the contractions to start again, but they never did. Suddenly, the silence was broken by an urgent bleeping noise from a machine above my head.

'What's that?' I was terrified now.

'The baby's heart rate is dropping,' the midwife said, scanning the machine attached to the pads on my belly. 'This baby is in distress.'

From then on, everything seemed to happen very quickly all around me while I looked on, helpless behind a fog of diamorphine. The room filled up with people and my legs were placed in stirrups. The bottom of the bed was whipped out from under me and a voice said: 'We're going to get your baby out now. We're going to give you a ventouse delivery.'

Ventouse? Putting a suction cup on my baby's head?

'Oh, God! Glen?' I called out, petrified.

'I'm here!' Glen appeared by my head and grabbed my hand.

'It's going to be okay,' he said, though he must have been as frightened as me. I couldn't feel a thing down there but almost a second later I saw the doctor whisking a tiny body away from the bed.

There's no crying! Why can't I hear the baby crying? Oh my God – is my baby dead?

'Waaah Uh Waah Uh Wahah Uh...' Tears sprang to my eyes when I first heard that strange hiccuping cry. Glen and I looked at one another in amazement: *Alive! Thank God, our baby was alive!*

'A beautiful, healthy little girl,' the doctor said from where he was still working on me as one of the nurses placed my baby on me.

As I looked down at her, her little face scrunched up and her perfect eyes closed, I was filled with an overwhelming happiness. I wanted to hold her, to touch her soft, new skin, but my body wasn't working properly – I couldn't even lift my arms and my eyes kept rolling back in my head. Down below, the doctor was still stitching me up. Now my eyes were drawn to the bloodstained sheets beneath me. God, there was so much blood everywhere! So much blood... My head felt woozy, my vision began to swim; I felt like I might pass out at any moment.

'Glen, our baby... Please take her.'

Gently, he plucked our child from where she had been lying on my chest.

'Do we have a name yet?' one of the midwives asked.

'Yes,' I breathed, my eyes now closed. 'It's Susanna – she's called Susanna.'

I was so exhausted then, I fell straight to sleep.

Susanna. Susanna... I repeated her name over and over in my head as I watched her in the see-through crib from my bed. I'd managed to get a few hours' sleep and when I woke up, I was amazed to see this perfect little creature by my side. Fine, dark hair framed a sweet little face and then, when her eyes popped open, I saw they were a startling bright blue. She looked like a perfect china doll.

Are you looking at me, Susanna? I wondered as her little pupils flitted around the room. I knew babies couldn't see in the first few days but even so, my little girl seemed so alert. We had come up with the name six months before, while on holiday in Tenerife. Though we didn't want to find out the sex of our child, I knew that if she was a girl, I wanted a name that had some reference to my mum, Susan. But it was tricky because I didn't want it to be exactly the same: this child needed her own identity. It was Glen who had suggested Susanna. It was perfect! Susanna May Wright had been born on 18 February at 5.10pm weighing 7lb 1oz.

No one could prepare me for the first terrifying six months of my baby's life. I felt like I was on high alert the whole time. It struck me that I had brought this tiny life into the world and now I had the overwhelming responsibility of looking after her. She was so small, so fragile! *How could I possibly do this?* No wonder my mother had felt so protective of me all the time. Glen had a couple of weeks off, but because we were now relying on his income, very soon he had to go back to work. He had sold his courier company a year earlier and was now in the painting and decorating business.

Alone in the house with my tiny child, I began to feel horribly anxious all the time. She was amazing, this little baby of mine: a precious gift. But at the same time I was acutely aware that this incredible gift could be taken away from me at any time. I'd stay awake, watching her sleeping for hours, fussing around as I checked to make sure the room was the right temperature and she wasn't in any danger. If she made a noise, I went to check on her; if she made no noise, I went to check on her, and if *we* made a noise, I went to check on her too. I was up and down like a bloody yo-yo! It was madness, but a kind of rational madness, I thought to myself. I had certainly never known worry like it. Sleep deprived, anxious and stressed, I thought a lot about my mum in those first few weeks, especially during the lonely early hours of the morning. I knew this was what she had gone through with me and I prayed that I would one day come out the other side, more or less intact. At times, I was just overcome with sadness that she couldn't be there with me to share the special moments with Susanna and I'd sob my heart out. Other times, I was filled with anger. *Where was she?* She should have been by my side. I wanted her more than ever before.

I breastfed Susanna from the word go and this gave me a very strong bond with my daughter from the start. That feeling of being connected to another person so deeply, it was wonderful, and reminded me that I had probably only had this once before in my life, with my own mother. Now I had it again! Still, I found it difficult to go from working full-time to being at home with a baby all day long. It was long, gruelling, demanding and often boring. At least at work you knew what you were doing from one hour to the next; it was all set and organised. With a baby you never knew where you stood!

I'd find myself wanting to take Susanna out for a walk and then, just as I'd got all her bits together in the buggy, she'd soil her nappy and start crying. Then as soon as I'd changed her, she'd demand to be fed and then I'd be stuck indoors for the next two hours. It was very frustrating. Just taking a shower felt like a major achievement and meals were usually eaten on the hoof, either while she slept or balanced on my knee as I burped Susanna on my opposite shoulder.

'How are you feeling, love?' Nan Floss asked me one day when I managed to get round to see her.

'Oh, you know… tired, stressed, constantly anxious…' I replied drily.

She looked at me hard: 'I'm worried about you.'

'Oh, Nan!' I wanted to reassure her. 'Look, I'm fine, really. All new mums get like this, surely? Show me a mum with a three-month-old baby who isn't sleep-deprived and sick with worry, and I'll show you a liar. It's normal. I'm not going to become agoraphobic like Mum did. Really, you don't have to worry about me.'

'That's motherhood,' Nan sighed. 'Trust me, it doesn't ever change – you just worry about different things.'

After three months I found a part-time nursery place for Susanna and went back to my bookkeeping job as Glen was now struggling to find work. He had decided to retrain as a tiler, but in the meantime money was tight. I thought a lot about my mum in that first year with Susanna – although I adored my daughter, I knew that life could have been so much better with Mum by my side, helping me and giving me advice. Sometimes, if I saw a grandmother in the street with her child, I'd boil over with rage.

John Dickinson! He stole so much from me.

And despite my reassurances to Nan Floss, I was secretly quite concerned about my own mental health. I could see now how the worry had driven my mother mad. I'd never had anxiety attacks before, but now I could be out having a normal day when suddenly I'd be gripped by a paralysing and utterly paranoid fear that something terrible was about to happen to Susanna and my whole body would freeze in fear.

One time I was round at Nan Floss's house and she was sat at the table peeling potatoes. The knife flickered and flashed menacingly in the light and I was mesmerised by its sharp blade. I sat there, unable to take my eyes off it, the panic inside slowly building.

The knife! The knife is dangerous. Something's going to happen to Susanna with the knife, I just know it. I know it. Got to do something. Got to do something...

'Nan,' I was breathing hard now. 'Please put the knife down. Please. Just put it away. We're going home soon and then you can do the potatoes.'

Of course as soon as I'd calmed down I realised there was nothing to get worked up about but at the time my fears were so real, so debilitating. Even my dreams were haunted by terrible thoughts and deadly fears. One recurring nightmare was of my grandmother pushing Susanna's pram into a pool of water. I heard myself shouting in the dream: 'What are you doing, Nan? Stop pushing her into the water. Stop!'

But I was always helpless to prevent the inevitable. Nan kept pushing the pram until it was fully submerged underwater and I'd wade in, trying desperately to find her. I'd be looking and looking, shouting out, 'Where is she?' but she was gone. Then I'd wake, drenched in sweat and crying my eyes out. And for the rest of the day I couldn't shake off that horrible feeling of doom, of being unable to keep my baby out of danger. So when the nursery suggested they take her swimming, I couldn't let her go – I knew it was just a dream but I was adamant I didn't want her in the water without me.

'What if something happens?' I said to Glen, trying to justify my fears. 'I mean, what if they get distracted and they're not watching her?'

As she grew older, the panic eased. I decided to take Susanna to swimming lessons myself as I wanted her to be able to cope in the water, and she loved it! She was actually a very energetic and athletic little child. I saw that she too was going to be sporty.

'What about another one?' Glen asked me one day.

'I don't know, Glen,' I murmured. Susanna was now coming up to three and she was the apple of our eye. Could I cope with another?

For a long time I resolved never to have another child because of the trauma of Susanna's birth. But as the years passed, I thought it would be selfish of me to deny my daughter the experience of a sibling. If she had a brother or sister, she would have someone she could rely on throughout her life, no matter what happened to Glen or me. I recalled my own childhood, the loneliness and silence of being an only child for so long. By the time my brother Terry had come along, there was such a big age gap we didn't have a strong connection. But childbirth had been so awful! I firmly believe I should never have been given the diamorphine when I was already so far gone.

'If we do this then I'm going to do it all differently,' I said to Glen. 'For one thing, I'm never taking that drug again.'

'Too right!' Glen agreed. He had been very angry at the time with how the staff coped with my birth. 'Those birth plans are stupid – you just do what feels right.'

I fell pregnant straight away this time. It was no fun going through the all-day morning sickness again, but at least I was a little more prepared. I carried the same as before – like a football stuck onto the front of my stomach – but this time I was convinced it was a boy.

''Fraid not,' the sonographer said as she moved the cold probe of the ultrasound over my belly. 'No, you've got a little girl in there.'

'Are you sure?' I asked. We hadn't wanted to find out the sex the first time around, but this time we were less romantic about the birth and more practical. It made sense to know in advance in case I had to go out and buy clothes for a boy.

'Quite sure,' she grinned. 'Girl.'

Glen and I exchanged proud smiles. Of course we didn't mind either way and another girl was going to be lovely!

In the end, the birth was just as quick as the last time but far less traumatic. I had spent all morning on 1 October 2006 at a soft play centre with Glen and Susanna, running around the different levels, going down slides and climbing up ladders. I was just lolloping over a rope bridge when suddenly I felt the unmistakable wave of pain building in my womb. My contractions had started! For a while, we didn't react. We carried on playing and even got ourselves a spot of lunch, but as wave upon wave of pain crashed over me, I realised it was probably time to go to the hospital.

'My waters haven't broken,' I puffed to the nurse on the

desk, wincing and holding onto the edge of the desk as I breathed in and out. 'But I've been having contractions for ages and they're…. ooh… pretty… pretty bad now!' I knelt down and let the high point of the contraction pass before popping up to the top of the desk again. Glen rubbed my back sympathetically (we had dropped Susanna round at Glen's mother Alison's house).

Rather annoyingly, when the duty midwife arrived she said I looked fine, pretty far from actual labour.

'Yeah? Well, I'm having a lot of pain so I think you better check me!' I insisted, determined to stand my ground. This time around I was more assertive and confident in dealing with the nursing staff. I was thirty years old and I knew my body – they didn't! Sure enough, the midwife nearly fell off her stool when she checked and found I was over 8.5cm dilated. Now the pain was very intense and it seemed to be getting worse every minute.

They put me in a delivery suite and invited me to get on the bed.

'No, thanks,' I said, puffing hard. 'I'm going to do this my way.'

We put on the stereo we had brought in with us, I opened all the windows to let in the air, and I walked around. We had taken a big medicine ball in with us and bouncing on that relieved the pressure for me. This time around the only pain relief I had was pethidine – 'gas and air'. Another technique, which relieved the more severe pain, was pressing my back up against Glen. After an hour or so, my waters broke and that's when the midwife finally insisted I get on the bed. I got up, and in record time, she was out and in my arms. I felt elated, amazing – like I could run a marathon! She was gorgeous, just as beautiful as Susanna, and we had our name ready: Isabelle Amy Wright.

It was all so different the second time around. From the start, I was confident and in control and this meant the panic and anxiety was kept to a minimum. Glen, too, was more relaxed and between us we seemed to cope more easily with the tough demands of a newborn baby. I was so happy with my little family and every day I felt blessed to have two gorgeous girls to love and cherish. It had been a rocky start, but now I loved being a mum.

I can do this, I told myself. *I'm a good mum and I'm determined to enjoy every single second!*

CHAPTER 23

BACK TO SCHOOL

'Bye Mum!' Susanna called as she raced out of the door, her spotty mac flapping in the wind.

'Bye, love!'

'Bye, bye, Mummy!' Little Isabelle toddled over to where I was hunched over my books at the kitchen table. She reached up and wrapped her arms around my neck, planting a big, sloppy wet kiss on my cheek.

'Bye, bye, honey,' I giggled, removing the saliva with my sleeve.

'We'll be back this afternoon around four-ish, I should think,' said Glen, as he hunted round the house for his car keys. I pointed to the kitchen counter and he made a grab for them.

'Don't rush back!' I smiled ruefully. 'I've got an essay to hand in next week.'

'Good luck!' he grinned, and he kissed me on the forehead before stooping down to pick up Isabelle.

'Come on, Babycakes! Let's get out of here and let Mummy do her work.'

'Thanks,' I sighed, before turning back to my books.

A second later, the door slammed shut, but by then I was already deep into my work.

The decision to return to my studies had been helped by colleagues at the Fun Club, who had told me that if I went back to school, I would automatically qualify for childcare funding. This meant I could study for my Early Years NVQ Foundation course without having to give up work. My colleagues agreed it would be a great boon to the club if I returned to my studies, and best of all, the most successful students would be given the chance to go on to study at university. For me, it was a no-brainer. I had always wanted to go back to school and now I was being offered the chance to do that while still being able to pay my bills. By now I had given up bookkeeping as I couldn't manage that and the demands of Fun Club while also looking after my own children. Fortunately, Glen's tiling business quickly took off and so between that and the club, we kept our heads above water.

As soon as I started the course, I loved it. I had picked up so much from the experience of working with kids, but now I was learning the theory and the science behind what we were doing. It felt great to use my brain again and though I was nervous when I had to write my first essay, the positive feedback I got was incredibly motivating. I recalled I had enjoyed English at school and it didn't take long for me to get back into my writing stride. Sometimes, it felt as if I could even express my thoughts better on the page rather than out loud. I worked hard – slipping in hours of study at night after the kids had gone to bed, at the weekends or very early in the morning – and was rewarded by passing my NVQ with distinction.

Consequently, I was offered the undergraduate place at Hertfordshire University to study for a degree in Early Years and Educational Studies. I was over the moon! There was never any question in my mind that if I was offered the place, I'd take it. After all, Glen was fully supportive and there was never going to be another opportunity like this again. Educational Studies was a subject I was passionate about and I relished the chance to acquire more knowledge. So in 2009, at thirty-three, when my youngest was just three years old, I started my university degree.

It was so exciting! I was put in a friendly group of mixed-age students, some of whom were much older than me, and because we were all a bit older and had chosen to be there, everyone was keen to learn. I still ran Fun Club most days but on Wednesday, I had a full day at university for my lectures and tutorials.

In the end I got quite good at managing my study time. When I wasn't on Mummy Duty or working at the kids club, I used every available opportunity to study. Today was a perfect example – Glen had offered to take the girls swimming in the morning and then they had a friend's birthday party in McDonald's at lunchtime. The plan was that they would visit their grandparents after lunch, which would give me at least five hours to make a good start on my essay. I glanced at the clock – 10.30am. With so many demands on my time, I needed to make the most of every minute. My mantra now was: *Let's crack on!*

Today's subject was the value of outdoor play and I had to write an essay on the various ways it could advance learning. It was just up my street! Even as a young girl, I had loved being outdoors and all the new research chimed with my instincts about the value of playing out of the house. When you are outside, all your senses are sharpened. You hear, smell and see things better than in artificial light. I read up on the new studies and was fascinated by their findings; I learned that when children play outside, they are more likely to play in bigger groups with mixed sexes and ages.

This information had already helped me to improve the setting at the Kids Club in so many ways. Back at work, I reinvested our earnings in new scooters, balls and sports equipment. We had a beautiful outside space that even included a woodland area, and from then on, I made sure the kids played in the woods too.

It felt like everything in my life was coming together – my work, my studies and my role as a mum. By now I was militant about sending my girls outside to play, even when the weather was less than wonderful.

'But it's pouring!' Susanna objected one day when I offered to take them to the park.

'There's no such thing as bad weather,' I reminded her, 'just bad clothing. Get your raincoats and your wellies on and you'll be fine!'

Life was so busy now, I hardly thought about my past, but I got a nasty reminder halfway through my first year at university: a letter from the Victims Unit of Hertfordshire Probation Trust. They had some shocking news. John Dickinson had committed an offence while he was let out on licence and now he was locked up in a psychiatric hospital. They didn't say what he had done, but as a result, he had been diagnosed with a serious psychiatric condition. In conclusion, the probation service said it was unlikely he would ever be let out again.

I finished reading the letter and let out a big sigh. For a moment, I just stood there, my mind buzzing, my emotions swirling inside me. On the one hand, I was pleased he was locked up and relieved he had been diagnosed with a clinical disorder, because of course, it had always struck me that there was something very wrong with him. On the other hand, I wondered about the value of his life, given he had spent the majority of it locked up at the taxpayer's expense, having committed some truly heinous crimes. Why was he still alive? To me, it didn't feel fair. Unlike my mum, he could still look out of a window and see the trees, the grass and the sky. I sighed and filed the letter away in my drawer, determined not to waste too much time thinking about him. After all, I had a life to live and more important things on my mind – my children, for one thing!

Something had changed inside me since I had become a mum. I had these two beautiful, lively girls and I wanted so much for them in the future, a future without pain and fear. It was so important to me that they had a regular home life with a mum and dad who cared for them and wanted the best for them. Nothing extravagant and fancy – God knows we couldn't afford it! They just needed a place where they could be themselves, so I made sure that their home was their sanctuary, a place where they could express themselves freely without fear of being teased or reprimanded.

Frequently I'd put on some fun music and we'd just dance around the living room, messing about and enjoying ourselves. In those moments, I was the happiest person on earth. We'd jump and shimmy, spin and bop till we were exhausted. Both girls were in gymnastics classes and they were so agile and graceful, it was amazing. I'd take them by the hands and swing them round the living room until we all collapsed in a heap on the floor. It was wonderful! But after those exquisite moments of joy, I'd always be left with a feeling of dread. I dreaded what would happen the moment they stepped outside the house, fearful of the people they would bump into or the situations they might find themselves in without my watchful eyes on them. In my mind, every situation was potentially life threatening and I found it very difficult to leave them in the care of others, even those I loved and trusted. My mind was constantly assaulted by all the many, terrible possibilities that might happen in my absence. *What if they get left in a car? What if a stranger grabs them while they're walking down the street? What if they get run over?*

All these dark thoughts crowded into my head until, like a sand timer slowly filling up, I was flooded with fears and worries. When I stopped them going out with their friends or joining a birthday party group in town, I could sense their frustration and confusion. 'I don't want to be like this!' I wanted to scream. 'I don't want to be the kind of mum that wraps them up in cotton wool!'

It was no good – I knew I needed to find a better way, a healthier balance in my own head. Even though Glen was always supportive and never challenged me when I let my worries overtake my reason, as time went on, he questioned my decisions. Why couldn't he take the girls into town? Why couldn't he take them to the park? It made no sense, he said. And I knew he was right. I was determined not to let my fear ruin their childhood. There came a moment when I decided I had to fight it, to let go of the panic which until now had hampered my abilities to be a good mum. It wasn't a sudden thing. There was no one event that changed my outlook, but I'm pretty sure it was after I got that letter.

Gradually, it sunk in that John Dickinson was a sick man and he had no right to dictate the way I brought up my kids. Day by day, I learned to let go a little more, to push my boundaries so that I wasn't constantly worried about them. *It's an amazing world out there*, I told myself every day. *Don't make them fearful of it. Give them the tools to be strong and independent on their own so they can go out there with confidence.* I knew what I had to do. It didn't come easy at first but over time, I started to relax more and it felt good to watch them grow and flourish as a result.

I couldn't believe it when I got a First! Although I knew a lot of my module work had been quite good throughout the year, I thought I was on course for a second-class degree. Then, when my exam results were posted online, I had to reread the numbers several times before allowing myself to believe it was true. Adding up the scores for each section, I realised I had just scraped a First. A First! *My God*, I thought to myself in wonder, *really clever people get Firsts. Was I clever, too?*

It was surreal, unbelievable and yet utterly wonderful at the same time. Until that moment, I had never felt clever in my life and yet I always knew there was some potential there, untapped, unexplored. Now, against all the odds, I had achieved a high degree at the age of thirty-six and I felt myself swell with pride. It meant so much to me, succeeding in my degree, with all the compromises and juggling I had to do. All those nights I just wanted to curl up on the sofa next to Glen or the Sunday afternoons I wanted to take my girls out to the Lakes or even visit my ageing grandmothers. I made sacrifices to educate myself, to better myself. I couldn't have done it without Glen of course, but no one else had written those essays for me – I had done it all myself. I had put myself through university and achieved a First Class Degree – yes, I had every right to feel proud.

'Say Cheese!' the photographer called out.

'Cheese!' we all chimed back obediently, grinning away like mad. It was 18 November 2011, and I had spent the last half an hour in the Alban Arena as the official photographer took my graduation portrait, with Glen and the girls by my side. Isabelle, now five, fidgeted with her red corduroy dress as she stood beside her eight-year-old sister, who wore a new grey dress and a dainty string of pearls around her neck. They both looked utterly adorable! The ceremony was being held in St

Albans Abbey later that day and we had decided to make a weekend of it, hiring a hotel room for the night so we could take our time, soaking up the sights of St Albans. I put my hand up to steady the precariously balanced mortarboard as it threatened to slip off my head again.

'So, how do you fancy a few outdoor shots?' the photographer asked. He glanced at his watch. 'We don't have much time but seeing as how you are all here, and your girls look so lovely, I'm sure we can take some nice shots behind the Abbey.'

'Yeah, that would be great. Thank you,' I said, gratefully. Already, it was such a special day and now we were being given the chance to make it even better.

Outside, on the large green lawns behind the Abbey, the last copper leaves clung to the branches of the trees and the bright winter sunshine brought natural smiles to all our faces. Susanna turned cartwheels on the grass and Isabelle spun in delighted circles until she collapsed in a bright red heap. We joked around and posed for pictures for the good-natured photographer, enjoying the chance of having some more 'natural' shots of the four of us together. In fact, we were having so much fun, we hardly noticed the time whizz by until the bells from the Abbey rang out across the town, signalling it was 2pm.

'The ceremony!' Glen shouted. 'It starts at 2pm. We've got to get down there. Come on!'

And with that, he picked up Isabelle, grabbed Susanna by the hand, and started off down the cobbled path towards the Abbey.

'Oh, blimey!' I shrieked. 'We're going to be late!'

And I picked up the hem of my long gown, put my hand on top of my head to stop the mortarboard slipping off again, and started to run after them. Somewhere behind us, we left the photographer, still fiddling with his camera.

'Good luck!' he called out after us.

'Thank you!'

It was a magical moment and one that I'll never forget for the rest of my life – the four of us running through the cobbled streets of St Albans together, my long black scholar's gown flapping behind me. Glen couldn't carry Isabelle the whole way so we all held hands together and flew down towards the Abbey, laughing with pure joy. It was crazy, beautiful and the most wonderful feeling in the world. The ceremony itself didn't even compare to those few precious seconds where we careered through the narrow streets, the four of us together on an exciting adventure. This was life; this was true happiness!

Despite all the setbacks I had suffered in life, I had done it! I had an amazing job, a brilliant husband, we had two gorgeous children and now I was an educated scholar too. At that moment I wished I could have gone back in time to tell my five-year-old self that it was all going to be okay, that she had all this to look forward to. I looked back to the fearful, anxious little girl who had grown up in the shadow of that terrible event and I wanted to put her mind at ease, to reassure her that despite all the confusion and uncertainty, she had a bright and beautiful future ahead of her. But I couldn't. I couldn't change the person I was back then and if I could, maybe I wouldn't have had the same drive and determination that I had now. Maybe those setbacks had served a purpose, made me the person I was today.

No, it was time to leave that little girl far behind and look to the future. All I could do now was show my own children that anything was possible if they put their minds to it. I wanted them to see my educational achievements, even at this late age. Yes, that one little piece of paper had great symbolic value for me: it was a turning point in my life, in my assessment of myself, and my sense of self-esteem. It told me that I was capable of so much, and from that moment I grew in confidence as a human being. Self-doubt was a thing of the past. I had faith now in my own instincts and abilities and this made me less worried and fearful. I started to look people in the eye when I walked along the street; I allowed myself to be more open to strangers where previously I had lived with a veil of fear between the world and me. Now I decided to lift that veil. The degree was just the first step on a journey of awareness and self-discovery. My outlook and horizons expanded and now, I felt confident to pick up books and talk to people and learn every day of my life. This was invaluable.

In fact, the degree made very little material difference to me. After graduation, I dived back into work and bringing up the kids. I loved my job running Fun Club so much that I never considered changing it or trying to land a position further up the managerial chain of command. It wasn't about that. For me, studying was much more personal. It was about fulfilling a promise I had made to myself many years before.

Now I had one more challenge to face: I had to confront my dad about the choices he had made when I was a child.

261

Even if it threatened our relationship, I had to find out why he had let the situation between Diane and me get so terribly out of hand. His son Terry had taken his A-levels at school and then went on to university without any problems whatsoever. There was never any question of him having to pay rent while he studied, so why me? There was no anger left in me now, just curiosity. As a mother myself, I knew how strongly I felt about my kids and the lengths I'd go to give them opportunities to work towards a rewarding future, so I couldn't, for the life of me, understand what had happened to me.

CHAPTER 24

DAD

For a long time my relationship with my dad stayed on an even keel – he came round to see the girls, or I popped by his place for a cup of tea. We chatted generally – small talk, really – and left it at that. I never brought up the past and neither did he. I didn't feel it was necessary to rock the boat or confront him when it had taken so long to get back together. It was all too painful, that part of our lives, and I knew he would do anything to avoid a conversation about Diane or how she had treated me. We kept it civilised but as a consequence, I always felt slightly awkward around him, never truly at ease, and that saddened me because we had got on so well when I was a little girl. In the end, I decided there was nothing else for it: for the sake of moving on and putting that all behind me, I had to try and find some answers to the questions that still haunted me.

The opportunity finally presented itself when Diane filed

for divorce. Although they had been separated for more than ten years already, they hadn't got round to divorcing. Now, she wanted to remarry, so her name kept cropping up in conversation with Dad. In fact, it seemed like she was causing stress all over again.

'She's trying to get three quarters of the value of the house!' he exploded on the phone one night. 'Can you believe it? She says she gave up her career to care for you.'

'Ha! Some caring!' I said.

'She wasn't very nice to you, was she?' said Dad quietly.

'No, she wasn't, Dad. She wasn't nice at all.'

'How about you write a statement for my lawyer saying that?' Dad suggested. 'I mean, I don't want her to get away with this because it just wasn't true.'

I let a long silence fall between us now. *Write a statement for him? What did he think I was going to say?* He was just as culpable as she was in all of this.

'Amanda?' his voice broke through my thoughts.

'Yeah, I'm here, Dad.' It was now or never – if ever there was an opportunity to confront my father about how he had treated me back then, this was it.

'Okay, well, I have to think about this, Dad,' I started. 'You do know that if I write a statement it won't reflect very well on you, will it? I mean, Dad, I always wondered why didn't you stop her? I'm your daughter. You never stuck up for me.'

Now there was another long silence. I felt myself holding my breath, desperate for his answer. *It was finally happening! We were finally having a conversation I'd imagined many times in my head.*

'I... I didn't want to rock the boat,' he finally stammered.

'What do you mean, Dad?'

'You had already lost your mother, your home, everything you had known before. I didn't want to split the family up, I just wanted to smooth it all over – keep everything nice. If I had divorced Diane and we'd lost the house, who knows how it could have ended up! I was terrified they would take you away and put you in care.'

'So you let her carry on treating me horribly because you didn't want to lose the house?'

'No, no, no! That's not what I meant. Look, at first, everything was okay. Diane was fine with you, remember? Okay, so she was never going to replace your mother, but your relationship was all right. It only got worse as you got older. I suppose it was so gradual I didn't even notice at first and as I say, it felt like I couldn't disagree with her or she'd get very angry, so I just went along with things, to make for an easier life.'

'Hmmmm... go on...'

'Then your brother came along and of course now we were a proper family so it got harder and harder to challenge her. I didn't want her to go off and take Terry with her, which is what she threatened to do when I didn't support her. She had me over a barrel – I was stuck.

'When you got to be a teenager, she said it wasn't right for us to be kissing and cuddling anymore. She made me feel bad about something which I thought was just, well, natural. It wasn't right of her but you know, maybe she was jealous of you or something? I don't know. At the time, I was wary of being seen to be doing the wrong thing. I came in for a lot of stick, you know, when your mother was killed. Your Chalkley family, they said things about me… And I had to fight so hard to keep you. It was all very painful, Amanda.'

'Did they blame you, Dad, for what happened?'

'Yeah, I think that's a fair way of putting it. They blamed me because I left your mum, and in their minds, if I'd never done that, she'd still be alive now because that bastard would never have got in the front door.'

This was so much information at once and I struggled to take it all in. I could see how hard it was for Dad. It was the most truthful and important conversation we had had in years and there were certain things we needed to say to one another.

'It wasn't your fault, Dad,' I sighed. 'Nobody could have seen what was coming, nobody was responsible for that man except himself.'

'Yeah,' said Dad. 'Yeah, I realise that, but it didn't make things any easier. Didn't stop me wondering myself if… if… well, if it could have been different somehow. Oh, I don't know! I was so young – I didn't know what I was doing.'

'They took you to court,' I said, recalling the terrifying day Nan Eve had dropped me off at school with the ominous warning that I might end up in care if things went badly.

'I know… I know…' Dad sighed. I could picture him now at the other end of the phone, his head in his hands. Still, I pushed on. Now that we were talking – really talking – I wanted to get to the bottom of it all.

'Why did they have to do that, Dad?'

'It was the social worker,' he spat bitterly. 'He told me that while you were settling in at The Paddocks, it was probably a good idea to keep the other side of the family away. You know, to let you get properly settled. I don't know why he said that and frankly, in hindsight, I don't think it was very good advice.

'I don't think they would have told me to do that sort of thing today. But, like I said, I was young – this was a totally shocking situation for which I was not prepared. I followed the advice of the so-called experts. I did what they told me. To me, the most important thing was making sure you were happy. Trust me, I never did anything to harm you, Amanda. Everything I did, everything, was for your best interests.'

Could this be true? I wondered. I tried to put myself in Dad's position. He had been determined to hang on to me, that was for sure, and I recalled so many happy memories of us together when I was a little girl. Back then, he had so much time for me – taking me to the playground or to the swimming pool, talking to me about his thoughts and ideas about being a vegetarian. Still, my mind kept returning to that last unbearable year at home when Diane refused to feed me or do my laundry. My father, who had brought me into the world, he had gone along with this.

'You know, she said awful things about my mum to me,' I said sadly.

'Who, Diane? Listen, I only found that out later. I suppose I didn't really know how bad things had got between you until it was too late.'

'Dad, she stopped feeding me!'

'You had both your nans…'

'No, Dad! Feeding me wasn't *their* responsibility, it was *yours*.'

'Yeah, yeah, I know. You're right. I'm sorry. I let you down, Amanda. I shouldn't have let her do that.'

Tears sprang to my eyes – hearing him apologise meant a lot to me. It couldn't change the past, or erase my memories, but I knew that from that moment on our relationship would be stronger, better for a bit of honest communication. I had said my piece, got it off my chest, and all I wanted to do now was move on.

'It's no good burying your head in the sand, Dad.'

'Yeah, I know. I know that. I could have done a lot of things differently. But I didn't, and I'm sorry. I could have been a better dad. I tried, Amanda – I really did.'

'Yeah, I know. And it's okay. Really, it's fine.'

And it was.

After that conversation, I thought a lot about what Dad had said and I suppose it all started to make sense. By the time I was a teenager the pattern in his marriage was already well established and nothing could have prevented the deterioration of my relationship with Diane except the end of their relationship. She had chipped away at his relationship with me, undermining it at every turn, even to the point where innocent signs of affection between the two of us were turned into a weapon to hurt my father. No, she had him over a barrel, always with that last trump card of being able to take Terry away from him if Dad upset the apple cart. Perhaps he knew that all along – he was only hanging on for the sake of Terry and me. Did he do the right thing? Was he just trying to ensure we both had a stable family life? As a mother myself, I knew that it was very hard to do the right thing all the time. Sometimes, out of a skewed sense of love and protection, we hurt the people we love most.

So, yes, maybe he could have done more to defend me, but I couldn't change the past and at least I understood now. I survived, and as an adult, I think I turned out okay. It could have been so much worse. I have a greater appreciation now for my father, for what he did for me. I know that, ultimately, he acted out of love and nothing else. In the end, I wrote the statement for him. I was always going to – after all, he is my dad.

CHAPTER 25

GOOD
VERSUS EVIL

In the course of writing this book, I decided to try and find all the evidence I could on my mother's death so I went to the local library and looked up all the old cuttings from the *Stevenage Comet*. I was truly shocked by the number of front pages that had been devoted to the story, which had unravelled slowly over the course of several weeks as the police made one awful discovery after another. First, there was the report of a tragic house fire that had killed a young woman. Then came the news the following day that after a post-mortem, it was found my mum hadn't died in the fire but had been strangled. The fire wasn't an accident: it was a deliberate attempt to conceal a murder. Then there was a manhunt for the murderer, followed by the news that the local park keeper had been charged with the crime, and a few months later, the awful reports of Dickinson's defence

271

in court. Finally, and thankfully, there was news of his conviction.

It was extremely shocking to see these very personal details of my childhood played out so publicly in the newspaper. There were pictures of me recovering at home after the fire and distressing interviews with my Nan Floss in the immediate aftermath of the murder, when she was in the darkest and most terrible throes of grief. It was difficult to read these reports and yet very important for me to do so, in order to finally put my mind at rest. It was the small details I was after, the information to fill in the blank spaces in my memories which had never really added up. As an adult, I wanted the full picture. I knew I was strong enough to find out the truth. For one thing, I never understood how the milkman had known about the fire. To me, it had appeared like a little fire on the end of the bed. Now, reading his testimony from the court, it all started to make sense.

Michael Knowles, the man who saved my life, told the judge at St Albans Crown Court that he had seen smoke billowing from the bathroom window of my house while he was on his way to work and heard my screams.

'I decided to knock down the door because it seemed to be urgent and I kicked it down,' he explained. 'The girl was three quarters of the way up the stairs and I ran and collected her.'

He took me to my neighbour's house, where apparently, I told him my mum was still trapped inside the burning house. Then, in an extraordinary act of bravery, he returned to the deadly blaze to try and find my mother.

'I got almost to the top of the stairs,' he told the court. 'I'm afraid I could not get any further because of the heat but I did try to raise anybody that was there.'

The trial judge praised Mr Knowles for his great presence of mind and later I found he was given an award for his bravery, but he was really a very modest man and he didn't want any fuss made. In the article, BRAVERY AWARD FOR MILKMAN, there was only one quote from him: 'Now, I just want to forget the whole thing.' It had obviously been a terribly distressing event for this quiet, unassuming man. It was left for his wife Maureen to say: 'We are all very proud of him.'

Reading Michael's testimony filled in the missing pieces of the jigsaw for me. I didn't ever recall getting off the bed and leaving my mother to go downstairs but I must have done. It made me sad to think that I left her there, but I suppose, on reflection, I needed to get off the burning bed in order to save my own life. I didn't remember screaming either, but once again, I must have done because it saved my life.

Now I knew too why nobody had questioned me about the murder. It all made sense: Michael Knowles didn't find me in the bedroom, he found me on the stairs, so the police must have assumed I had been in my own room or somewhere else in the house when my mother was murdered. And that I had not been a witness to what happened. Perhaps with all the trauma of what I went through they didn't want to question me too hard, only asking whether I knew what he looked like, not whether I had seen what he'd done or even experienced it myself. And that was why John Dickinson got away with two life sentences: one for murder and one for arson. Had it been known that he'd strangled me too, he might have been found guilty of a third offence: attempted murder.

There was no question about it: Michael Knowles was a true hero. Not only did he risk his life to save mine but he also went back inside the house, running an even greater risk, to try and help my mother. I had always wondered how he had known to come into the house, thinking there was just a small fire on the bed. Now I knew that the fire had grown much bigger, to the point where it was obvious from the road that the place was in flames. It saddens me greatly, but at one point, when I was twelve, I had an opportunity to meet him and I didn't go because I was scared. I was confused about what I would say to him and I was frightened of bringing up the memories of what happened on that day. Now, as an adult, I regret not meeting Michael Knowles because I know he has now passed away and I dearly want to shake his hand and thank him for everything. I do hope his family, his children and grandchildren know what a fine, upstanding man he was, not just because he saved my life, but because he also shaped my view of the world.

It has always stayed with me, the thought that one man destroyed a life that day, while another man saved a life. They both came to the same house, my house in Colestrete, with two different intentions in their hearts: one evil, the other good.

And so, if I ever felt in doubt about the essential qualities of mankind, I would think of Michael Knowles. Mankind isn't all bad, I reasoned, when there are people like him in the world. There is a balance here, the capacity for great good and great evil in all of us. And whenever there is a bad situation, there will always be great acts of goodness and kindness to follow.

I think about this a lot in these worrying times. Whenever I hear news of a terrible terrorist atrocity, I think about the two men who changed my life: John Dickinson and Michael Knowles. Always, in the wake of these crimes, you hear incredible stories of hope, rescue and pure acts of love and kindness. Men and women who go out of their way to shield others from harm, to save lives or simply comfort the dying, even when it means risking their own lives. Good will always follow evil – I know this for a fact. You've just got to hope that if you're in a tragic situation the good people will be there for you. Admittedly, it doesn't always happen. The cases of poor children who are abused in their homes and have no hope of rescue make me very sad. But while there is hope in my heart I will not lose my faith in the essential goodness of people to overcome evil acts.

And what turns people into killers in the first place? This is something that has occupied my thoughts for a good many hours over the years. I've read up a lot and thought deeply about this question because obviously it is one that has shaped my life. What is the underlying reason for someone being able to or wanting to kill another human? Is it their childhood? Is it just something innate within them? Or is it a sense of power they are after?

For many years I looked into this and it was only when I started to study at university that I bumped into a concept which I felt offered the most comprehensive answer. It was called 'attachment theory' and it was used to explain how the early stages of attachment in a baby and a child could subsequently affect their future behaviour as an adult. The central idea was quite simple: a baby needed to develop a relationship with at least one caregiver for that child's successful emotional and social development and to help them regulate their own feelings. So within a normal social setting a child growing up forms strong and deep bonds with their mother or father, allowing them to nurture and value future bonds with others. But, if a child doesn't make deep connections as an infant, their brain is wired differently: they can't form normal social bonds because they are not conditioned that way and they don't know how to control their own emotions. Therefore, they exhibit less social, more abnormal and even violent behaviour. So I believe that somebody like John Dickinson, for example, did not have a normal attachment model as a child, and there was a void where his social bonds should have been. It was perhaps this that turned him into a person who could take pleasure from killing.

The theory itself is much more complicated than that. I'm simplifying and perhaps I'm completely wrong. I continue to pay attention to changes in the fields of psychology that will help me to gain a greater understanding, not just of my past, but also of the way us humans work. I continue to grow and learn every day. Today, I am unsure whether I believe in God or an afterlife, but I do have strong morals and family values. I have faith in the greater good of mankind, and it's the here and now that we have control of and these decisions we make today will shape our future. We all have a sense of morality inside us, thanks to the bonds we share as human beings. And it is this that informs us of the difference between good and evil. So if I ever feel despairing or despondent about the future of our race, I think of Michael Knowles. I think of the unassuming milkman who passed by a child in need and refused to look away.

CHAPTER 26

A MOTHER'S
LOVE

A strange thing happens when your parent dies young. At some point you become older than they were when they died and from there, you go past them. Locked in time, they are forever young. My mum didn't live beyond the age of twenty-five and now, here I am at forty years old, a much older woman than she ever was, with more experiences in every area of life. Somewhere along the way, my perception of Mum changed: like a parent myself, I became protective of her. I look back at myself at twenty-five and I cringe at the memory of the things I said and did. At that age, you are only just learning how to be an adult; you're finding your feet. It's all new and peculiar and you make mistakes because that's what you have to do in order to learn how to do things better. I have passed my mother's final age of her life and it makes me feel sorry for her, in the way a mother might feel for a child. At forty, I represent the sum of all my experiences, so my judgements are sharper, my decisions better and my core beliefs are stronger than ever. It will sadden me forever that as the years pass and I embrace a richer and deeper understanding of life, my mother will never experience the same. She will always be twenty-five.

So I project onto my mother's memory the future I wish she had been left to enjoy. I think about the way she loved to ride horses and I tell myself that if she were alive today, we would go horse riding all the time. The truth is I have never ridden a horse, though I am determined in my forties I will learn to ride. I tell myself that in this day and age she would have received effective treatment for her depression; she would have been alleviated of her suffering, and then she would surely have shaken off the agoraphobia to enjoy all the delights of the world outside. I imagine that she would have learned to drive and that her opportunities would have expanded hugely, helping to fight off any further bouts of depression.

My mother was a creative individual, a person who took great comfort in self-expression, and therefore I tell myself that her poetry would have found a receptive and appreciative audience. I tell myself about the joy she would have felt, knowing and sharing in the lives of her beautiful granddaughters, and I tell myself that no matter what happened, we would have had a wonderful relationship. I can see it all and the further I get down this road, the more unjust and tragic it feels that she was robbed of all these possibilities. I know my mother would be happy if she lived today.

There is so much that makes up a human life – not just the work we do, the people we love or the things we learn. There is the vast inner world we occupy and some are blessed with the talent to share their world with others through art. Okay, so maybe my mother was depressed, and at twenty-five, her life hadn't worked out exactly the way she wanted, but that wasn't the end of her story. During her depression she thought very deeply about things and as a consequence, she grew as an individual. Being depressed and at home doesn't mean you're not travelling in life. It just means that the journey isn't so obvious to everyone else. I wonder where would she be now, had she been given the chance to live on?

Over the years, I have thought a lot about my mother's depression and what it meant. I worried that I would inherit it, or that it might be passed on to my kids, so I made sure that exercise and healthy living were always integral to our lives. I've never really drunk alcohol and I don't do any drugs, mainly from preference, but also because I'm aware of how these substances can affect your mood, emotions and perceptions. So far, I'm pleased to say, I don't think any of us exhibit signs of mental ill health, but I don't take it for granted. I am aware that we could be at greater risk than others.

I have now been in my job for seventeen years and have no inclination to do anything else. When we first opened our doors, there weren't any after-school clubs like ours in the area. We pioneered what was, back then, a new idea and over time we have developed it in creative and exciting ways. At our maximum capacity we can take forty kids, run holiday clubs and employ eight members of staff. We even provide meals Monday to Friday and I'm hugely proud of what we have created. The club is always for the kids and here, away from the rules and expectations of school and family life, I watch them thrive. Here, they are free. They can relax and be themselves. It is a setting I hope feeds their creativity and confidence. This job is a very important part of my life and it helps to shape the person I am today. I try to be a good role model for the children, so I think a lot about the way I behave and the things I do. For as long as it makes me happy, I will keep doing it.

Sadly, both my Nan Floss and Nan Eve now suffer with dementia. It started two years ago for both of them, when they were in their eighties, but has progressed differently for each. While my Nan Floss is still able to live in her own house, being cared for by my cousin Claire and her son, my Nan Eve is now in a specialist dementia home as her condition means she can't take care of herself. Before she went into a home, Nan Eve explained that she bitterly regretted the custody battle over me when I was young, but they had been advised by social services not to let my Aunty Carol and her family see me in the immediate aftermath of the fire as it would unsettle me. Carol obviously thought they were losing me and that's how it ended up in court. It was all so stupid and I hope now families of bereaved children are getting better advice from social services.

I try to see both of my wonderful grandmothers as often as possible, to show them the same love and care that they have given me all these years. It is sad to see them both getting so confused and mixed up, forgetting things that have happened and people they know and love. With this condition there are good days and bad – you just take the good days when you can and accept the bad. I still see my dad and have a good relationship with my half-brother Terry. I haven't seen or spoken to his mother Diane since the day I left home. Meanwhile, my daughters continue to bring me endless joy, while my husband is a constant source of love and support.

As I said when I started this book, this is not a sad story: it's a story of hope and survival. Since I was dragged out of the burning building where my mother so cruelly lost her life, I have done more than just survive – I have thrived! I am living proof that good will overcome evil, hope triumphs over despair and there is nothing so strong as the human spirit.

And I have these things – I *am* these things – because of one person: my mum, Susan Lowson. Because of the love she showed me when I was first a baby and then a child, because of that deep attachment, I was able to overcome the tragedy that blighted my early years. A child never forgets love. It starts from when you are just a tiny baby. A mother's love takes care of all a baby's needs: feeding, drinking, changing nappies, clothing, nurturing and encouraging a child to walk and talk. This attachment makes social bonding possible in the future. Even when that love is taken from them, a child will have the imprint of these bonds in his mind, enabling him to grow up emotionally healthy and strong, proving that ultimately, a mother's love can never be truly broken or forgotten.

A military friend recently told me that soldiers that have been shot or wounded on the frontline often call out for their mothers. Big strong men in their dying moments on earth call out for their mums. In all the carnage and atrocity that surrounds them it's only their mothers that they want. That is the strength and purity of a mother's love; there is nothing quite like it.

I have been without the physical presence of my mother for all these years and yet I still feel her love for me, stronger than ever before. Floss talks about my mum a lot too, about how she was such a gentle, caring person and how she was a good mother. It comforts me that she can still remember her daughter, despite the dementia, and the affection in her voice always echoes that in my heart. Recently, Floss emptied out a cupboard, where she found some poems and letters my mother wrote. Reading those poems, penned so many years before, gave me the idea to write this book. Mum's poems have given me a great deal of comfort through the years. They kept me strong throughout my life. I could look at her poems when I felt sad and know that she kept going even when she had bad days because she loved me, and that I had to keep going and being strong for her. I wanted to show that she had not died in vain, that something good could come out of her death. I wanted to share my mum with the world and to give her back a life through words, even if she could never have it on earth. And finally, I wanted to say thank you.

So thank you, Mum, for all the love you gave me and I still feel to this day. You will forever be in my heart. The last words, the ones you wrote for me, are your own:

MY CHILD
Her sunny little ways on these depressing days

A MOTHER'S LOVE

Her cheerful cute smile that spreads for a mile
Her cheeky grin my heart can win
Her sweet little voice that makes such a noise!
Her happy face, with gift of grace,
For my child of love, I give thanks to above.

By Susan Lowson

ACKNOWLEDGEMENTS

There are so many people I would like to thank, it is hard to know where to begin. So let me first start by saying thank you to the police and to the judiciary, and all the people who worked within that organisation when this crime was committed. You did an incredible job, quickly capturing and jailing the culprit. This prevented other innocent people being put at risk of harm or death from an evil, cold-hearted predator.

I would like to thank all the hospital doctors and nurses who carefully and skilfully treated my burned legs.

Thanks to the caring milkman Michael Knowles, who courageously saved my life.

A special thanks to Nan and Grandad Lowson, who took me into their home after I left hospital. All my needs were taken care of in a warm and loving environment.

Thank you to my father, who provided for me and kept me

fit and active by walking and swimming most weeks. I'm glad you taught me to swim.

Thanks to my Aunty Carol and Uncle Mick and my cousins Greg and Claire – you all invited me to stay at your house most weekends and cared for me. Growing up, your family house parties were the best, and we danced our cares away through the night. Carol, thanks for teaching me to ride a bike – I'm still cycling weekly!

Thank you to my Nan Floss; we often walked and talked together and we had the best conversations. I was saved once but you also saved me by always being there for me. Our bond was so strong, it saw us both through the tough times.

Thanks to my cousin Greg, who helped me when my life was falling apart at the seams. You offered me a way out when I needed it most.

Special thanks to my Aunty Jane and Uncle Keith for all the help and support you have both given me over the years. Thanks for being there.

Thank you to all the staff and children of Fun Club. Having the opportunity to work with children in a lovely setting with wonderful staff was a turning point in my life. My dear colleagues are some of my friends and make going to work every day worthwhile and enjoyable. Thanks to Linda (who has left, but stays in touch), Joy, Paula, Yasmin, Natasha, Ferdousi, Manjit, Carol, Ann and Angela. And a special thanks to Tina for her constant hard work and support.

Thank you to my husband Glen; you have always cared for and protected our family unit. You have a big warm genuine d I love you with all of my heart. The children couldn't ked for a better dad.

Thanks to my beautiful, wonderful children, Susanna and Isabelle. I love you so much, my heart could burst: you have made my life complete. As a family we share so many special memories and have so many to look forward to. Thanks to my husband and children for giving me my first family home where I feel I truly belong and which has given me hope for the future.

And to all my extended family and friends who have been there for me, and for all the laughs. Thanks to Donna and Pat, Kieran and Julie, Kelly and George, Stephanie and Ben, Gill and Ian, Angela, Kim, Cheryl and Sally.

A special thank you to Katy: you believed in the story and made an idea a reality. Your friendly, warm persona and expertise as a writer define you as a truly remarkable person.

Last, but not least, I would like to thank my mother for giving me life and caring for me when I was a baby and a young child. You did your best and you would have done more if your life had not been cut short. For all that we had together, and for all that we would have had together, thank you. There was so much more to give. Your words from your poems have given me strength and hope from afar. I will never forget you, my distant star.

Love,

Amanda x

MY MOTHER OF BEAUTY, MY DISTANT STA[R]

Your heart was true
But your head was a muddle
At times life was hard
A bit of a struggle
You loved to go horse riding
To gallop and trot
Moments of pleasure
All your fears you forgot
We would go to the park
On the slide and the swings
Over the lakes we would walk
And you spoke of your dreams
To publish your poems
For us to go riding together
These dreams were cruelly taken
But your poems I will treasure
Through all the hard times
You never gave up on us
You stayed by my side
It was you I could trust
Together against the world
Our bond was strong
So sadly out of our hands
It all went wrong
Your words are a beacon of hope from afar
I will never forget you
My mother of beauty, my distant star.

By Amanda Wright